ALSO, BY DR. DERRICK WASHINGTON

THE JOURNEY TO VICTORY SERIES

From Trials To Testimony

&

Walking in Victory

I0540440

 About the

Journey to Victory Series

Faith Over Fear: Armor for the Anxious: Winning the War in Your Mind with God's Word and Peace is part of **The Journey to Victory Series**—a powerful three-book collection written for those who are walking through pain, waiting, and personal transformation. The series began with *From Trials to Testimony*, which explores how our deepest struggles can become the very story God uses to bring freedom to others. It continued with *Walking in Victory*, a guide to moving from survival into purpose after the storm.

Now, in *Faith Over Fear: Armor for the Anxious*, Dr. Derrick Washington equips readers to confront internal battles with the spiritual weapons God provides. Each book in the series offers biblical encouragement, practical application, and soul-renewing truth to help you walk faithfully through life's hardest seasons—and emerge victorious.

FAITH
OVER
FEAR
ARMOR FOR THE
ANXIOUS

Winning the War in Your Mind with
God's Word and Peace

DR. DERRICK WASHINGTON

"I am leaving you with a gift—peace of mind and heart. And the peace I give is a gift the world cannot give. So don't be troubled or afraid."

— *John 14:27 (NLT)*

Faith Over Fear: Armor for the Anxious: Winning the War in Your Mind with God's Word and Peace

For permissions or inquiries, contact: Inspiring Faith by DW Ministries derrick.washington36@gmail.com
First Edition, 2025 ISBN: 979-8-218-78141-5 (Paperback)
Printed in the United States of America
Cover and Interior Design: Inspiring Faith By DW
For permissions, inquiries, or speaking engagements, please visit:
www.inspiringfaithbydw.com

Dedication

*To my **wife, Sharon**—your faith, love, and strength have anchored me through every storm.*

*To my **children and grandchildren**—you are the legacy I'm honored to fight for.*

To every heart that has wrestled with fear in the silence,

To the weary warrior still standing despite anxiety's weight,

And to the next generation who will walk in peace because you chose to break the cycle—

This is for you.

You are not alone. You are armed with peace.

To my Savior, Jesus Christ—You are my shield, my sanity, and my shalom.

Foreword

By Rev. Dr. Hoszel West, Jr.

In a world full of fear, doubt, uncertainty, and internal unrest,
Faith Over Fear: Armor For The Anxious could not have arrived at
a more pivotal time. We are battling a spiritual war within
ourselves which challenges our thoughts and actions to spiral out
of control. On the outside of us it seems okay, but internally we
are drowning inside. This book is more than just a self-help guide.
It's a spiritual survival manual written by someone who has lived
the battle, and has walked out in victory!

Dr. Derrick Washington has written a timely and
heartfelt work that equips The Body Of Christ to confront the lies
of anxiety and doubt, and replaces it with the firm truth of God's
Word! With compassionate wisdom and biblical insight, he takes
the readers by the hand, page by page and walks them through the
spiritual battlefield of our lives-one thought at a time. Dr.
Washington doesn't just offer solutions and strategies, but
Scripture-soaked armor- that reminds the reader that healing is not
found in desensitizing, ignoring, or managing the fear within, but
by facing it with the power of the Holy Spirit.

This resource is not a theory, but it is truth forged through challenging trials. Dr. Washington has lived the content of this book-through his seasons of physical affliction, mental wrestling, and spiritual warfare. You can feel every ounce of passion throughout the pages of every chapter written! My prayer is that this spirit-driven work becomes more than a resource- it becomes a refuge and rallying cry for every anxious believer!

Let's walk through this together—armor on, faith up, fear down. **You are not weak. You are not alone. You are armed with peace.**

— *Rev. Dr. Hoszel West, Jr., Good Hope Missionary Baptist Church*

Endorsements

"In a world full of turmoil and uncertainty that can lead to anxiety and fear, in *Faith Over Fear: Armor for the Anxious,* Dr. Derrick Washington gives a battleplan that can lead to perseverance and peace in the midst of life's internal storms. Combining personal insights with scriptural reinforcements, this book is ideally suited for personal devotion as well as small group discussion. Are you feeling anxious in some kind of battle today? There's armor waiting for you in *Faith Over Fear: Armor for the Anxious.*

— *Jim Lemons*, PhD, Professor of Theological Studies, Dallas Baptist University

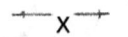

x

Preface

Anxiety doesn't knock—it crashes in. It whispers lies when we try to sleep, clutches our chest in moments of stress, and convinces us we're powerless against life's unknowns. I know this battle firsthand.

This book was born out of years spent fighting battles in the unseen realm. I've walked through dark valleys—wrestling with chronic illness, grief, spiritual attacks, and the mental exhaustion that comes when peace seems out of reach. But I've also discovered something powerful: we are not helpless. As children of God, we have been equipped with spiritual armor that can shield, strengthen, and secure us—even when the war rages within.

Faith Over Fear: Armor for the Anxious isn't a clinical manual—it's a spiritual call to arms. It's for the believer who loves God but feels overwhelmed. For the prayer warrior who is weary. For the anxious heart that needs to remember the truth of who they are in Christ.

This is your invitation to step into the reality of victory. Not because you're strong, but because God is. You already have the armor. Now it's time to learn how to wear it well.

— *Dr. Derrick Washington*

Abstract

Faith Over Fear: Armor for the Anxious:
Winning the War in Your Mind with God's Word and Peace

is a faith-based guide to overcoming anxiety by equipping believers with biblical truth, spiritual strategies, and practical tools. Rooted in Ephesians 6 and the full armor of God, this book speaks directly to those who wrestle with fear, stress, spiritual fatigue, or emotional unrest.

Blending theology with testimony, Dr. Derrick Washington draws from real-life experience and scriptural insight to unveil the lies anxiety tells—and how God's Word sets us free. Each chapter focuses on a specific battlefront, such as fear of the future, overthinking, emotional exhaustion, or spiritual warfare, and offers actionable steps to reclaim peace and victory.

The book includes:

- Biblical character studies and fictional snapshots for personal reflection
- "Common Lies We Often Live With" and "How to Fight Back" for each chapter
- Morning declarations and evening prayers
- A complete Scripture Index, tools for spiritual renewal, and a group study guide

Written for individuals, small groups, and ministries, *Faith Over Fear: Armor for the Anxious* offers a Christ-centered path toward lasting inner peace. Whether you're in the middle of a battle or helping someone through theirs, this book is a reminder that you are not alone—and you are not unarmed. You are fully equipped to win the battle within.

Contents

DEDICATION VI

FOREWORD.. VII

ENDORSEMENTS.. IX

PREFACE XI

ABSTRACT XII

HOW TO USE THIS BOOK... XVI

INTRODUCTION XVII

EXPOSING THE LIES THAT TRIGGER ANXIETY 1

PROTECTING YOUR WORTH WHEN YOU FEEL INSECURE 12

STANDING STEADY WHEN PANIC COMES 22

BLOCKING FIERY DARTS OF FEAR AND DOUBT 32

WINNING THE WAR IN YOUR MIND 42

SPEAKING GOD'S WORD INTO EMOTIONAL CHAOS 52

ACTIVATING PEACE THROUGH PRAYER 62

LIVING IN VICTORY, NOT IN FEAR OF THE NEXT ATTACK 72

DISCERNING THE ENEMY'S WHISPER 82

FIGHTING ANXIETY WHEN THE WORLD IS QUIET 91

GENERATIONAL ANXIETY AND SPIRITUAL PATTERNS 103

ESTABLISHING NEW RHYTHMS OF REST AND RENEWAL 112

RENEWING THOUGHT PATTERNS THROUGH THE SPIRIT 121

INTERCESSION AS A SHIELD 130

FINAL ENCOURAGEMENT: 141

YOU ARE ARMED WITH PEACE 141

INVITATION TO CHRIST: 143

YOUR VICTORY BEGINS AT THE CROSS 143

SPIRITUAL TOOLS & RESOURCES.. 145

PERSONAL SELF-ASSESSMENT 146

SCRIPTURE DECLARATIONS 147

INTERCESSORY PRAYER PROMPTS 149

SCRIPTURE INDEX BY CHAPTER 150

ABOUT THE AUTHOR.. 153

CONNECT AND SHARE YOUR TESTIMONY 155

How to Use This Book

This book is designed to be both a spiritual companion and a battle plan. Each chapter addresses a specific form of anxiety or inner struggle, offering biblical truths, reflection moments, and faith-filled prayers to help you actively renew your mind and walk in God's peace. Whether used as a personal devotional, small group study, or healing journal, you are invited to take your time—pray through each section, revisit the scriptures, and allow the Holy Spirit to lead you from anxiety to anchored confidence.

You can move through the chapters in order, or go directly to the one that speaks to your current need. Use the tools, journal prompts, declarations, and prayers daily as part of your spiritual rhythm. Let this be more than a book—it's your armor.

Introduction

We live in anxious times. The world feels heavier than ever. From health crises and financial uncertainty to fractured relationships and spiritual fatigue—our peace is constantly under pressure. But what if anxiety doesn't have the final say?

Scripture tells us that the weapons of our warfare are not carnal but mighty in God (2 Corinthians 10:4). That means anxiety is not just a feeling—it's a battlefield. And if it's a battlefield, then we need to be armed.

This book is designed to help you fight back—spiritually, scripturally, and practically. Each chapter explores one aspect of anxiety's tactics and God's counterattack: truth, prayer, worship, mental renewal, and more. You'll find biblical insight, real-life application, declarations, prayer prompts, and spiritual tools to equip you day by day.

Whether you're walking through overwhelming stress, facing long-term fear, or interceding for a loved one who is struggling, this book is your guide to standing strong. Not in your own strength, but in God's unfailing power.

You are not alone. You are not without defense.

You are armed with peace.

CHAPTER

The Belt of Truth

Exposing the Lies That Trigger Anxiety

Primary Verse:

"Stand therefore, having fastened on the belt of truth..."

— Ephesians 6:14a (ESV)

Introduction: When Anxiety is Rooted in a Lie

Anxiety often doesn't begin with fear—it begins with a falsehood. A whispered lie. A distorted truth. A seed of doubt planted so subtly that you didn't even notice it growing. Lies like: *"You're not enough." "God's distant." "You'll always feel this way."* These are not just anxious thoughts; they are arrows from the enemy. And without the **belt of truth**, we are left unguarded, vulnerable to deception.

In biblical times, the belt was the piece of armor that held everything together. Without it, the soldier's gear would fall apart. Spiritually, **truth** is what secures us. It grounds us. It protects us from spiritual disorientation.

In this chapter, we'll expose the lies anxiety loves to tell and replace them with the unshakable truth of God's Word. Because when you know the truth, anxiety starts to lose its grip—and freedom begins.

⚜ Theological Insight:
Why Truth Comes First

In Roman armor, the belt ("ζώνη" zōnē in Greek) was the centerpiece that held every other weapon in place. It was the first piece of a Roman soldier's armor—tightened before anything else could be held in place. The Sword, the breastplate, and the tunic were all secured by it. Paul lists it first because truth is foundational. Without it, everything else becomes unstable.

Spiritually, truth isn't just an idea; it's the foundation that secures every other weapon in your spiritual arsenal.

Truth brings stability. Without it, everything falls apart.

Spiritually, anxiety thrives where truth is loose, forgotten, or replaced by lies. This become evident in an atmosphere of distortion, half-truths, or fear-based assumptions. Because before you can walk in peace, hold your shield, or wield your sword—you need to be grounded in what's real. Truth isn't just informational—it's transformational. It brings alignment to our thoughts, emotions, and perspective.

The Lies We Believe

Anxious believers often rehearse the same destructive internal narratives. It often repeats silent lies:

- *"I'm not enough."*
- *"I'm alone in this."*
- *"This will never change."*
- *"God must be punishing me."*
- *"If I don't control everything, everything will fall apart."*

If you've ever felt your chest tighten before walking into a room, or rehearsed a conversation in your head a hundred times before saying a word out loud—you know what it's like to be ruled by anxious thoughts.

For some, anxiety whispers.

For others, it shouts.

For me, it usually came in the form of an internal voice that asked:

"What if you fail again?"

"What will they think of you?"

"You're probably not even supposed to be here."

It wasn't until I began recognizing that these **were not neutral thoughts**—they were **spiritually strategic lies**—that I realized I was in a battle, not just having a bad day.

Each of these statements is rooted in a **lie**—and these lies aren't just psychological—they're **spiritual strongholds**. The enemy uses them like invisible chains to bind your peace.

Truth breaks the cycle.

✖ Common Lies We Often Live With:

1. **"If I don't control everything, everything will fall apart."**
   Rooted in fear and perfectionism, this lie keeps you in a constant state of stress. But the truth is: *God holds all things together* (Colossians 1:17).
2. **"I'm bothering people if I ask for help."**
   Isolation thrives on this thought. But Scripture tells us to *"bear one another's burdens"* (Galatians 6:2).
3. **"I'll always be this way."**
   This is one of the most dangerous lies because it's

disguised as acceptance. But God specializes in transformation (2 Corinthians 5:17).

4. **"God is disappointed in me."**
   This one cuts deep. But in Christ, we are already accepted, already forgiven, already loved. (Romans 8:1)

My Breaking Point

There was a day I couldn't breathe. Not because I was sick—but because my thoughts had spiraled out of control. I remember sitting in my car, hands on the wheel, engine off, heart pounding, telling myself, *"You're fine. You're okay."*

But I wasn't. I had a full schedule. A full life. And an empty peace.

I realized then: I had been *agreeing with lies for so long* that I didn't recognize truth when I heard it. I had to go back to the Word—not just to read it, but to **believe it and speak it** until my soul caught up.

 Supporting Scriptures to Confront Lies:

1. **John 8:31–32 (ESV)**
   "If you abide in my word, you are truly my disciples, and you will know the truth, and the truth will set you free."

    Truth doesn't just calm anxiety—it breaks

chains. Freedom starts with knowing God's Word.

2. **2 Corinthians 10:4–5 (NIV)**

   "The weapons we fight with are not the weapons of the world... we take captive every thought to make it obedient to Christ."

   Our minds must become spiritual battlegrounds where we fight lies with divine truth.

3. **Psalm 119:165 (NKJV)**

   "Great peace have those who love Your law, and nothing causes them to stumble."

   Peace comes not from comfort, but from clarity—loving God's truth brings emotional steadiness.

Eve and the First Lie

In Genesis 3, Satan didn't use a sword—he used a **subtle question.** He didn't attack Eve with violence—he used deception:

"Did God really say...?" (Genesis 3:1)

That single twist of truth led to doubt, rebellion, shame, and ultimately fear. Lies **undermine trust** and **open the door** to emotional chaos.

Satan twisted truth just enough to make Eve question God's goodness. That's how spiritual anxiety begins: when doubt takes root where trust should live.

Just like Eve, many of us feel anxious when we think:
- God is withholding.
- God's promises don't apply to us.
- We have to fend for ourselves.

But the **truth** is:

"Every word of God proves true; he is a shield to those who take refuge in him."
— Proverbs 30:5

And He is for you, not against you (Roman 8:31).

Spiritual Warfare Teaching: Replacing Lies with Truth

The enemy doesn't need new tactics—he recycles the same lies because they keep working. You can't win the battle within if your inner dialogue is feeding the enemy's agenda.

But God has equipped us to **tear down strongholds** (2 Corinthians 10:4).

How to Fight Back:

1. **Identify the Lie**
   Journal recurring thoughts that heighten anxiety. What recurring anxious thoughts keeps tormenting you?

2. **Search the Scriptures**

   Ask: "What does God say about this?" Find a truth that contradicts the lie. (e.g., "I'm alone" → *"I will never leave you nor forsake you." – Hebrews 13:5*)

3. **Speak Truth Aloud**

   Faith is activated when truth is *spoken*, not just known (Romans 10:17). The enemy operates in silence. Break the silence with God's Word.

4. **Meditate on It Daily**

   Let truth become your emotional default. *(See Joshua 1:8).*

Faith in Action: Truth Exchange Practice

Create a chart like this in your journal:

Lie I've Believed	God's Truth
I'm not strong enough	*"His strength is made perfect in weakness." – 2 Cor. 12:9*
God doesn't care about me	*"Cast your cares on Him, for He cares for you." – 1 Peter 5:7*
I'm going to fail again	*"He who began a good work in you will complete it." – Phil. 1:6*

Transformation Starts with Truth

The Belt of Truth isn't something you wear once. It's something you **tighten daily**.

You don't always "feel" free when you speak truth. But over time, truth changes the narrative. It stops the spiral. It centers your soul in something stronger than emotion: the unshakable Word of God.

If you're anxious today, ask yourself:

- What lie am I partnering with?
- What truth have I neglected?
- What would change if I believed what God says more than what fear says?

 Warfare Prayer

Father,

I confess I've believed lies that feed my anxiety. Today, I take off the robe of fear and tighten the belt of truth around my life. Help me to identify and confront every distortion the enemy has spoken over me. Let Your Word be my foundation, my guide, and my peace.

In Jesus' name, Amen.

 Scripture Declarations

- ❖ "I walk in truth, not turmoil."
- ❖ "God's Word steadies my thoughts."
- ❖ "I will not partner with fear—I will stand in truth."

❖ "I am not my feelings—I am who God says I am."

❖ "God's truth is greater than my fears."

❖ "I will walk in peace because I am grounded in truth."

 Journal Prompt

What's one anxious thought you've believed for too long?
What Scripture truth can replace it?

Group Reflection Questions

1. Why does the enemy target our beliefs before our behaviors?
2. Which truth from today's Scripture stood out the most to you?
3. What's one way you can begin **tightening your belt of truth** this week?
4. Which lie do you think is most common among believers today?
5. Why is it so important to "speak" truth aloud?
6. What makes God's Word more powerful than your emotions?

CHAPTER 2

THE BREASTPLATE
OF RIGHTEOUSNESS

Protecting Your Worth When You Feel Insecure

Primary Verse:

"...and having put on the breastplate of righteousness."

— Ephesians 6:14b (ESV)

Introduction: When Insecurity Becomes an Identity

Insecurity doesn't always shout. Sometimes it whispers in silence. *"You're not good enough." "Why would anyone choose you?" "You messed up again—how could God still love you?"* These thoughts may sound like your own, but they often echo the enemy's agenda—to strip you of your confidence by attacking your identity.

That's why God gives us the **breastplate of righteousness**. Not self-righteousness. Not performance-based righteousness. But the kind that is gifted through Jesus—the righteousness that declares: *"You are covered, cleansed, and called."*

In Roman armor, the breastplate guarded the heart—the very place where worth is most often wounded. In spiritual battle, insecurity aims for your core. But when you wear God's righteousness, shame has nowhere to land, and comparison has nothing to cling to.

In this chapter, we'll uncover how to guard your heart with the truth of who you are in Christ, even when everything in you feels undeserving.

What Is the Breastplate of Righteousness?

The Roman breastplate, called the *thorax*, protected the heart and lungs—vital organs. In spiritual terms, Paul says righteousness is your **heart protection**.

But not self-righteousness. The Greek word here, *dikaiosynē*, refers to **divine approval or right standing with God**. It's not something you earn—it's something you receive through faith in Jesus (2 Corinthians 5:21).

When insecurity, guilt, or shame rise up, it means the breastplate may be loose—or missing. Many anxious Christians are under spiritual assault simply because they don't understand how *secure* they are in Christ.

Common Lies We Often Live With:

- "I'll never be good enough for God."
- "God only uses perfect people."
- "I need to clean myself up before I can come to Him."
- "My value depends on how others see me."
- "If I mess up, I'll lose His love."

These are not just insecurities—they are **spiritual deceptions** that erode your identity and leave your heart unguarded.

When Insecurity Feels Like Identity

For years, I wrestled with the quiet fear that I was never "enough." I'd speak with confidence in public, but inside, I was begging for approval. I was wearing a **mask of confidence** while my chest was unprotected.

That's what insecurity does. It tells you that:
- Your past disqualifies you.
- Your worth is performance-based.
- You have to earn God's attention.

But Scripture is clear:

"He has clothed me with garments of salvation; he has wrapped me with a robe of righteousness..."
— Isaiah 61:10 (CSB)

You don't fight anxiety by trying to prove yourself—you fight it by *remembering what Jesus already did.*

My Breaking Point

There was a day when I sat alone in my car after a ministry event, surrounded by people who clapped and shook my hand—but I felt like a fraud. I had just encouraged others, but I went home feeling empty.

God spoke to my heart in that silence:

"You are not righteous because of what you do. You are righteous because of what I've done."

That moment didn't instantly remove the struggle, but it began to recalibrate my heart. It reminded me: I don't perform for approval. I live from a place of already being loved.

 Supporting Scriptures to Strengthen the Heart:

1. **Romans 5:1 (NIV)**

   "Therefore, since we have been justified through faith, we have peace with God through our Lord Jesus Christ."

   Justification brings peace. Your anxiety may stem from forgetting you're already made right with God.

2. **Proverbs 4:23 (NLT)**

   "Guard your heart above all else, for it determines the course of your life."

   Righteousness guards your heart against false accusations and internal chaos.

   2 *Corinthians 5:21 (ESV)*

   "God made him who had no sin to be sin for us, so that in him we might become the righteousness of God."

This is not borrowed righteousness. It's your identity in Christ.

Moses — Insecure but Called

Moses, called by God to deliver Israel, responded not with faith—but with insecurity:

"Who am I that I should go to Pharaoh?" — Exodus 3:11

Moses questioned his voice, his background, and his ability. Sound familiar?

But God didn't boost his self-esteem—He declared His presence:

"I will be with you." — Exodus 3:12

When you know God's presence and righteousness are with you, insecurity begins to lose its voice.

 **Spiritual Warfare Teaching:**

Recognizing Accusation

The devil's name Satan means "accuser." His attacks are often personal and targeted:

- ❖ "You're a bad parent."
- ❖ "God's disappointed in you."
- ❖ "You'll always struggle with this."

But righteousness is your shield against condemnation:

"There is therefore now no condemnation for those who are in Christ Jesus." — Romans 8:1

You don't have to fight for approval—you fight from approval.

How to Fight Back:

1. **Guard Your Inputs:** Be mindful of voices that reinforce insecurity (social media, toxic relationships, even inner critics).

2. **Confess the Truth:** Don't just think it—say it. Speak who you are in Christ aloud.

3. **Dress Daily:** Just like you wouldn't leave the house without a shirt, don't walk into the world without putting on your spiritual armor.

Faith in Action: Speaking Righteousness Over Yourself

Create a habit of confessing your **God-given identity**, especially when anxiety hits:

Insecure Thought	Righteous Confession
I'm not doing enough	*"I am complete in Christ."* – Col. 2:10

| I feel too broken to be used | *"I am God's workmanship."* – Eph. 2:10 |
| God is angry with me | *"I am at peace with God through Jesus."* – Rom. 5:1 |

Repeat these aloud daily. The more you declare truth, the more your heart aligns with it.

 Warfare Prayer

Lord,

There are moments when I feel exposed, ashamed, and unsure of who I really am. I've allowed insecurity to speak louder than Your Word. Today, I choose to put on the breastplate of righteousness. Cover my heart. Silence the accusations. Remind me that I am deeply loved, fully forgiven, and already accepted in You.

In Jesus' name, Amen.

 Scripture Declarations

- ❖ "I am covered by the righteousness of Christ."
- ❖ "My heart is protected from shame."
- ❖ "I do not live for approval—I live from identity."

Journal Prompt

What is one area of your life where you constantly feel "not enough"?

What Scripture will you declare over that area this week?

Group Reflection Questions

1. Why is it important to understand the difference between self-worth and righteousness?
2. What's one false label you've worn that you need to take off?
3. How does knowing you're already approved change how you face your battles?

CHAPTER 3
THE SHOES OF
PEACE

Standing Steady When Panic Comes

Primary Verse:

"...and, as shoes for your feet, having put on the readiness given
by the gospel of peace."

— Ephesians 6:15 (ESV)

Introduction: When Panic Knocks You Off Balance

Panic doesn't ask for permission. It shows up uninvited—racing heart, tight chest, spiraling thoughts. One moment you're fine, the next your world feels like it's caving in. Anxiety has a way of knocking the breath out of your spirit and the ground out from under your feet.

But God gives us something powerful for these moments: **the shoes of peace**.

In Ephesians 6, these aren't ordinary sandals. They represent stability, readiness, and grounding in the Gospel of peace. Roman soldiers wore cleated footwear that gripped the terrain, giving them traction in battle. Spiritually, these shoes anchor us when fear tries to make us flee.

Peace isn't the absence of chaos—it's the presence of Christ in the middle of it. It means standing firm, even when everything in you wants to run. When panic tries to uproot you, God's peace becomes your footing.

In this chapter, we'll discover how to put on peace daily, prepare for anxious moments in advance, and walk through storms without slipping.

⚘ Theological Insight:

Gospel Shoes that Anchor You

In Paul's day, Roman soldiers wore hobnailed sandals called *caligae*. These were thick-soled, studded shoes designed for grip and stability on rough terrain. Without them, a soldier could be thrown off balance easily in battle.

Paul equates these shoes with the **gospel of peace**—not just peace as a feeling, but peace as a **foundation**. The Greek word *eirēnē* (εἰρήνη) means more than tranquility. It speaks of wholeness, harmony, and confidence because of reconciliation with God.

When panic strikes—whether from bad news, spiritual warfare, or internal fear—it's your **peace footing** that keeps you from falling.

✖ Common Lies We Often Live With:

- "If I have peace, I won't feel fear."
- "Real Christians don't get panic attacks."
- "I must be spiritually weak if I feel anxious."
- "Something must be wrong with me—I can't calm down."
- "God is disappointed in me when I feel overwhelmed."

These lies are subtle, but deadly. They plant shame where peace should grow. The truth is that **peace is not the absence of emotions—it's the presence of Jesus despite them**. You can feel fear and still choose to stand.

When Panic Hits Like a Wave

Panic doesn't always look dramatic. Sometimes it's subtle—a tight chest, racing thoughts, shallow breathing, a sense of being unsafe with no visible threat.

I remember standing in a grocery store line one afternoon, completely fine one moment—and then out of nowhere, a panic attack hit. My heart pounded. I couldn't catch my breath. I wanted to run, cry, scream—anything but stand still.

And yet, in that very moment, a verse rose up in me: *"You will keep him in perfect peace, whose mind is stayed on You…"* — Isaiah 26:3 (NKJV)

I whispered it. I repeated it. I stood on it. And eventually, the wave passed.

That's when I realized: **peace is not the absence of pressure—it's the presence of Jesus in the middle of it.**

The Floor Wasn't Moving—But I Was

There was a night during my recovery from illness when the world seemed to spin. I wasn't physically dizzy—it was anxiety. I sat in my bedroom and felt like the ground underneath me was unstable, even though it wasn't.

I remember grabbing hold of the arm of my chair and whispering through clenched teeth:

"God, I need Your peace right now—not tomorrow. Not later. Right now."

What came next wasn't instant calm—but a gentle steadiness. I began to breathe again. I began to **remember who He is**. And I realized—my shoes had been off too long. It was time to lace up the peace again.

Supporting Scriptures to Stand On:

1. **Isaiah 26:3 (NKJV)**
"You will keep him in perfect peace, whose mind is stayed on You, because he trusts in You."

Peace is a result of focus, not circumstance.

2. **John 14:27 (ESV)**
"Peace I leave with you; my peace I give to you. Not as the world gives do I give to you. Let not your hearts be troubled, neither let them be afraid."

Jesus offers peace that isn't shaken by external chaos.

3. **Philippians 4:6–7 (NIV)**
"Do not be anxious about anything, but in every situation...

present your requests to God. And the peace of God... will guard your hearts and your minds..."

Peace is a guard. It protects when you pray instead of panic.

Peter on the Water

Peter knew what it was to feel peace—and to lose it.

"Then Peter got down out of the boat, walked on the water and came toward Jesus. But when he saw the wind, he was afraid, and, beginning to sink, cried out..." — Matthew 14:29–30

Peter stood until he shifted his focus. The moment panic took over, he lost his footing.

But notice—**Jesus didn't let him drown.** He reached out and steadied him. That's what Jesus still does today: He resets our feet on peace when panic pulls us down.

Spiritual Warfare Teaching:
Peace Is a Weapon

We often think peace is passive. But in spiritual warfare, **peace is a defensive weapon** that protects your emotional footing.

The enemy wants to make you anxious so you'll become unstable.

"Let the peace of Christ rule in your hearts..."
— Colossians 3:15

When peace rules, fear can't. When peace reigns, panic recedes.

How to Fight Back:

Step 1: Pre-load Peace Verses

Don't wait until you're drowning—store peace Scriptures in your memory and phone notes.

Identify the Panic Pattern

Is it certain places, thoughts, or times of day that trigger anxiety? Track the pattern and be proactive.

Step 2: Practice a Peace Routine and Ground Yourself in Truth

When anxiety flares:

- Stop.
- Breathe deeply.
- Declare the verse out loud. Declare: *"God's peace rules in me. I will not be shaken."*
- Visualize the presence of Jesus beside you.

Step 3: Walk in Peace and Turn the Panic into Prayer

When panic whispers "You're not okay," respond:

"I may not feel okay—but I am held by the One who is."

"God, I stand on Your peace—not my perception."

Peace is not a luxury—it's your **battle footwear**.

Step 4. Keep Your Peace Shoes On

Peace isn't just for crisis moments. Wear it daily.

Begin your day with peace on purpose. Say:

"I put on the shoes of peace. I will not be shaken today."

- Start your day with a verse of peace.
- End your day with a prayer of gratitude.
- Make peace your preparation—not just your reaction.

Faith in Action: "Peace on Standby" Strategy

Create your Peace Toolkit:

- **Peace Verse** – Choose a go-to Scripture to repeat when panic rises. (e.g., Isaiah 26:3)
- **Peace Posture** – Practice deep breathing and repeating the verse aloud. Anchor your body and mind in God's truth.
- **Peace Plan** – Have a short prayer ready:
- *"Jesus, I stand in Your peace. Guard my mind. Ground my feet."*

These small tools help you **stand steady when the storm comes suddenly**.

🙏 Warfare Prayer

Prince of Peace,

There are moments when I feel unsteady, when anxiety rushes in and I can't find my breath. But You, Lord, are my anchor. You offer peace the world can't give and fear cannot steal. I choose today to put on the shoes of peace. Help me to walk boldly, even when panic tries to shake me. I receive Your presence and grounding grace.

In Jesus' name, Amen.

 ## Scripture Declarations:

- ❖ "My feet are fitted with the peace of the gospel."
- ❖ "God's peace guards my heart and my mind."
- ❖ "I will not be shaken—I stand on the Rock."

 ## Journal Prompt:

When do you feel most vulnerable to panic or fear?

What does God's Word say to you in those moments?

Group Reflection Questions:

1. What's the difference between worldly peace and God's peace?
2. Can you recall a time when you stood in peace during a storm?
3. What can you do this week to anchor yourself in peace more quickly?

CHAPTER4

THE SHIELD OF SALVATION

Blocking Fiery Darts of Fear and Doubt

Primary Verse:

"In all circumstances take up the shield of faith, with which you
can extinguish all the flaming darts of the evil one."

— Ephesians 6:16 (ESV)

Introduction: When Fear Feels Like an Attack

Fear doesn't always whisper. Sometimes it comes in like a fiery dart—sudden, sharp, and aimed at your deepest insecurities. Doubt follows close behind, questioning God's goodness, your purpose, or whether things will ever change. These aren't just fleeting thoughts; they're spiritual assaults designed to wear you down and make you retreat.

But God has given us a defense: **the shield of faith**.

In ancient Rome, a soldier's shield was not just defensive—it was strategic. Large and often covered in leather, it could extinguish flaming arrows. Soldiers even locked shields together for mutual protection. Faith works the same way. It not only blocks the enemy's attacks, but also reminds us we're not alone—we fight alongside others and under God's covering.

This chapter will teach you how to lift your shield when the battle heats up, how to recognize lies launched at your heart, and how to extinguish fear before it takes root. Faith doesn't eliminate the fire, but it makes sure it doesn't reach you.

⚜ Theological Insight:

Faith is Your Defense

Paul tells us to *"take up"* the shield of faith. That means it's not automatic—you have to **actively choose** faith in moments of spiritual attack.

In ancient warfare, Roman soldiers carried large, rectangular shields (*scutum*) made of layered wood, metal, and leather. These shields were often soaked in water before battle to extinguish **flaming arrows**—the enemy's psychological and physical weapons of fear.

Spiritually, those flaming darts are **accusations, lies, sudden fear, doubt,** or **temptation** that aim straight for the heart. When panic hits or fear tries to paralyze, the **shield of faith stops it midair.**

✖ Common Lies We Often Live With:

- "If I had stronger faith, I wouldn't feel afraid."
- "Real Christians don't struggle with doubt."
- "Fear means I've failed spiritually."
- "God must be disappointed in me for being anxious."
- "If I trust God, I shouldn't have these thoughts."

These are not just personal doubts—they're fiery darts the enemy uses to keep you paralyzed and ashamed. But the truth is:

faith isn't the absence of fear, it's choosing to trust God in the middle of it.

When Fear Feels Like Fire

Fear doesn't always whisper—it often screams. You wake up with your heart racing before the day even starts. Your phone rings, and dread fills your chest.
You get unexpected news, and your first thought is: *"I can't handle this."*

These are **spiritual darts**—and they come suddenly.

I remember getting a medical diagnosis that stopped me in my tracks. My mind spiraled into worst-case scenarios. But in that moment, a small but powerful verse came to mind:

"I will not be afraid of bad news; my heart is steadfast, trusting in the Lord."
— Psalm 112:7 (NIV)

It didn't mean the situation wasn't real. But my **faith response** created a *shield* to stop the fire from spreading.

The Night I Slept Clutching a Promise

There was a night I sat in my car outside the emergency room—too weak to move, too uncertain to drive away. I had just spoken with a nurse who urged me to come in immediately. My oxygen levels were dropping. The words "COVID pneumonia" echoed in my ears like a verdict.

My chest felt like it was caving in. Breathing took effort. Every inhale was a battle.

In that moment, a flood of fear crashed over me:

What if I wait too long?

What if I don't recover from this?

What if this is how it ends?

Panic tried to grip me—but so did a deeper truth. A quiet whisper pushed through the noise in my soul, reminding me of Psalm 46:1:

"God is our refuge and strength, a very present help in trouble."

I whispered it to myself over and over again. I clung to it like air. I walked into that ER with trembling legs and labored breaths—but covered in divine strength. I wasn't fearless. But I was *not* alone. And that made all the difference.

 Supporting Scriptures to Fuel Your Shield:

1. **Hebrews 11:1 (ESV)**

   "Now faith is the assurance of things hoped for, the conviction of things not seen."

   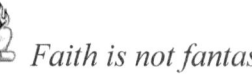 *Faith is not fantasy—it's firm assurance, even in the unseen.*

2. **Psalm 91:4 (NLT)**

   "His faithful promises are your armor and protection."

God's Word becomes your shield when you trust in it.

3. **Romans 10:17 (NKJV)**

   "So then faith comes by hearing, and hearing by the word of God."

   The more Word you consume, the stronger your shield becomes.

David vs. Goliath

David didn't carry a physical shield, but his faith shield was **massive**.

Everyone around him was paralyzed by Goliath's threats. But David declared:

"You come to me with sword and spear… but I come to you in the name of the Lord." — 1 Samuel 17:45

His boldness wasn't in himself—it was in **who he trusted**.

Faith doesn't deny the size of the enemy—it magnifies the **power of God**.

Spiritual Warfare Teaching: The Shield Moves With You

Unlike the helmet or breastplate, the shield is **mobile**. It can be lifted, lowered, aimed in every direction. That means:

- You must be alert to incoming attacks

- You must stay *active* in faith, not passive
- You must cover *others* with your shield too (like Roman soldiers did when they locked shields together)

How to Fight Back:

1. **Name the Dart**

   What lie or fear is hitting you right now?

   - Financial ruin?
   - Rejection?
   - Health crisis?
   - Future uncertainty?

2. **Raise the Shield Intentionally**

   Faith is not automatic. Take action:

   - Read God's promises out loud.
   - Memorize key Scriptures.
   - Surround yourself with faith-filled community.

3. **Soak Your Shield Daily**

   Just like Roman soldiers soaked their shields in water to extinguish fire, soak your heart in God's Word. Worship, study, and prayer saturate your spirit and prepare you for battle.

4. **Lock Shields with Others**

    Call a friend or spiritual mentor. Join a small group. Ask for prayer.

    Faith isn't meant to be wielded alone.

Example Shield Declaration:

"This fear is loud, but God's Word is louder. I lift up my shield and stand behind His truth today."

Faith in Action: "Shield Up" Strategy

Next time fear rises:

1. **Name the Dart** — Is it fear of failure? Abandonment? Sudden bad news?

2. **Raise the Shield** — Speak a verse aloud.

3. e.g., *"God has not given me a spirit of fear..."* – 2 Tim. 1:7

4. **Stand Firm** — Choose trust even when emotions say otherwise.

Faith says: *"I trust God more than I fear this."*

 Warfare Prayer

Father,

Fear often fires arrows into my heart before I can even brace for them. But You have given me a shield. I raise my faith in You right now—not because I feel strong, but because You are strong.

Let Your Word be the wet leather that extinguishes every lie, every worry, every fear. I stand behind Your promises, and I choose to believe even when it's hard.

In Jesus' name, Amen.

Scripture Declarations

- ❖ "My faith is a shield—fear will not overtake me."
- ❖ "God is my refuge and defense."
- ❖ "I will not be afraid of the fire—my God is with me."

Journal Prompt

What fear has been launching darts at your heart this week? What truth can you use to shield yourself from it today?

Group Reflection Questions

1. What are some common "flaming darts" you've faced recently?
2. How do you know when your shield is strong—or when it's slipping?
3. Who can you help "cover" this week with your shield of faith?

CHAPTER 5

THE HELMET OF SALVATION

Winning the War in Your Mind

Primary Verse:

"Take the helmet of salvation..."

— Ephesians 6:17a (ESV)

Introduction: When Your Thoughts Turn into a Battlefield

Anxiety doesn't always start with a circumstance—it often starts with a thought. One stray worry can spiral into panic. A passing doubt can snowball into despair. That's because the mind is the battlefield where most spiritual warfare begins. And without protection, it's easy to believe every anxious thought, assume the worst, or forget who you are in Christ.

That's why God gave us the **helmet of salvation**.

In battle, a Roman soldier's helmet wasn't optional—it was essential. It protected the head, the most vital and vulnerable area during hand-to-hand combat. Spiritually, our helmet guards our mind with the truth that we are saved, sealed, and secure. Salvation isn't just a past event—it's a present defense.

This chapter will show you how to put on that helmet daily, how to renew your mind with truth, and how to silence the lies that try to overtake your thinking. The enemy may aim for your head— but your identity in Christ keeps you covered.

Theological Insight:
Salvation Protects the Mind

The **helmet** (*perikephalaia* in Greek) was a thick, metal piece covering the Roman soldier's entire head, cheeks, and jaw— providing critical protection for the brain. Without it, a blow to the head could mean instant death.

Spiritually, the **helmet of salvation** protects your mind from destructive thoughts, doubt, confusion, and identity crisis. It reminds you that **you are saved**, **secured**, and **set apart**—even when your emotions say otherwise.

Anxiety often begins in the mind: "What if...?" "Why did...?" "Will it always be like this?" These looping thoughts can **spiral quickly into panic, fear, and despair**. But salvation brings **clarity**, **confidence**, and **mental covering.**

✖ Common Lies We Often Live With:

- "If I really trusted God, I wouldn't be anxious."
- "I can't control my thoughts—they control me."
- "I'll always be stuck in this mental pattern."
- "God is tired of my overthinking."
- "I'll never be free from racing thoughts or panic."

These are not just random ideas—they are spiritual attacks launched at the **mind**, which is the control center of your life. **The helmet of salvation reminds you that you're not a victim of your mind—you are a victor through Christ**.

The Battle of Thoughts

Anxious people often fight silent wars. No one can see it—but the mind is loud.

I used to wake up already in the middle of a mental fight:

- *"How am I going to get through today?"*

- *"What if I mess this up?"*
- *"I should've handled that better yesterday."*

Overthinking became a habit. Anxiety became a routine. Until I started **putting on the helmet of salvation intentionally** every morning—speaking out who I am in Christ and what He's already done.

I wasn't fighting for peace—I was and still am learning to fight *from* salvation.

Racing Thoughts in a Silent Room

I remember lying in bed, lights off, house quiet—yet my mind was louder than a freight train. I replayed conversations. I anticipated arguments. I worried about things that hadn't happened—and might never happen.

Sleep felt like a luxury I couldn't afford.

But one night, after weeks of this pattern, I remembered a verse I'd memorized in childhood:

"You will keep him in perfect peace, whose mind is stayed on You…" — Isaiah 26:3

I got out of bed, placed my hand on my forehead, and said aloud:

"Lord, I receive Your helmet of salvation. Let peace guard my brain tonight."

That moment didn't erase every anxious thought. But something shifted—because **the Word of God was no longer just in my memory; it became my mental armor.**

 Supporting Scriptures to Guard the Mind:

1. **Romans 12:2 (NIV)**

   "Do not conform to the pattern of this world, but be transformed by the renewing of your mind."

    Spiritual transformation happens when your mind is renewed by truth.

2. **1 Thessalonians 5:8 (CSB)**

   "Put on the helmet of the hope of salvation."

   This helmet isn't just about defense—it's about hope.

3. **2 Corinthians 10:5 (ESV)**

   "Take every thought captive to obey Christ."

   Your mind is a battleground. Don't let enemy lies run free.

Elijah — The Prophet Who Mentally Collapsed

In 1 Kings 18–19, Elijah had just called down fire from heaven. But soon after, he fled in fear. Isolated and exhausted, he said:

"I have had enough, Lord. Take my life." — 1 Kings 19:4

This was a **mental collapse** under spiritual and emotional pressure.

What did God do?

- He fed Elijah (physical restoration)
- He allowed rest (emotional reset)
- And then He **spoke truth to him** (spiritual renewal)

Sometimes, what your mind needs most is **divine truth** gently spoken into the chaos.

⚔ Spiritual Warfare Teaching:
You Can Choose Your Thoughts

You can't always control what enters your mind, but **you can control what stays**.

That's why we take thoughts captive—not just to stop negativity, but to replace it with *truth*. Salvation gives us:

- **Security** in our identity
- **Clarity** in confusion
- **Hope** in despair
- **Authority** over tormenting thoughts

🗡 How to Fight Back:

1. **Identify the Mental Patterns**

   Track your most common thought spirals. Are they:

   - Catastrophic ("What if everything goes wrong?")

- Self-critical ("I always mess up.")
- Spiritually anxious ("What if I'm not really saved?")

2. **Intercept and Replace**

Don't just rebuke thoughts—replace them with truth:

- Write down Scriptures that directly counter your fears.
- Declare your identity out loud.

3. **Create a "Helmet Habit"**

Each morning or before a mentally heavy situation:

- Lay hands on your head and pray God's Word over your thoughts.
- Listen to Scripture audibly while getting ready.
- Say: "I am saved. My thoughts are secured in Jesus."

4. **Memorize a Mental Anchor Verse**

Here are some great ones to choose from:

- 2 Corinthians 10:5 – "I take every thought captive."
- Philippians 4:8 – "Think on what is true, noble, right…"
- Romans 8:6 – "The mind governed by the Spirit is life and peace."

Faith in Action: "Helmet On" Morning Practice

Each morning, before your phone, your email, or the news:

1. **Speak your identity:**

   "I am saved, loved, secure, and covered."

2. **Declare a verse aloud:**

   "I have the mind of Christ." – 1 Cor. 2:16

3. **Pray against mental attacks:**

   "Lord, cover my thoughts. Let no lie live in my mind today."

This is not ritual. It's **armor**.

 Warfare Prayer

Lord,

You know how loud my mind can be. Thoughts race. Doubts scream. Fear circles my logic and my memory. But today, I put on the helmet of salvation. I declare that I am Yours. My mind belongs to Christ. No lie, no attack, no voice of shame or worry has permission to stay. Guard my mind with peace. Anchor my thoughts in truth.

In Jesus' name, Amen.

 Scripture Declarations

❖ "My mind is guarded by God's truth."

❖ "I wear the helmet of hope and salvation."

❖ "I have the mind of Christ and I will not fear."

Journal Prompt

What thought pattern causes you the most anxiety?
What Scripture can help you take that thought captive?

Group Reflection Questions

1. How do you know when your thoughts are under spiritual attack?
2. What's the difference between knowing you're saved and applying salvation to your daily thoughts?
3. What can you do daily to "put on" the helmet of salvation?

CHAPTER 6
THE SWORD OF
THE SPIRIT

Speaking God's Word into Emotional
Chaos

Primary Verse:

"...and the sword of the Spirit, which is the word of God."

— Ephesians 6:17b (ESV)

Introduction: When Emotions Feel Louder Than Truth

There are moments when anxiety isn't quiet—it's deafening. Fear floods in. Emotions spin out. Logic feels far away. In those moments, we don't just need comfort—we need a weapon.

That's where the **Sword of the Spirit**, which is the Word of God, comes in.

Unlike the other pieces of armor, the sword is both defensive and offensive. It not only protects—it strikes back. When Jesus was tempted in the wilderness, He didn't argue with the devil or reason His way out—He quoted Scripture. Every time. That wasn't coincidence. It was strategy.

This chapter will equip you to do the same. Whether your emotions are spiraling, your peace is under attack, or lies feel overwhelming, God's Word is your weapon. You don't have to stay silent in spiritual chaos. You can speak—and shift the atmosphere.

Theological Insight:
The Word Is Your Weapon

Until now, every piece of armor we've studied has been **defensive**. But the **sword of the Spirit** is different—it's a **weapon**. It's how we go on the **offense**.

The Greek word used here for *word* is *rhema*—not just the written word (*logos*), but the **spoken**, specific, personal word of God. This is **Scripture declared aloud** with faith, in response to a situation or attack.

Why does that matter?

Because anxiety often speaks **loudly and irrationally**. Emotional chaos spirals when we think silently but don't **fight back verbally**. The enemy wants you quiet. But **God wants you armed.**

✗ Common Lies We Often Live With:

- "I'll always struggle with this."
- "I've already tried—nothing works."
- "God's Word works for others, not me."
- "My emotions are too powerful to overcome."
- "I don't know enough Scripture to fight back."

These lies aim to **silence your spiritual voice**—to convince you that you're unarmed, unqualified, and defeated. But the truth is: *you are not empty-handed—you are sword-equipped.*

When Emotions Speak First

There have been moments when my emotions tried to dictate my truth:
- *"I'll never get out of this."*
- *"I've failed too many times."*

- *"God is silent—maybe He's distant."*

These thoughts don't just passively float through your mind—they try to take **root** in your spirit. And that's when the **sword of the Spirit must be drawn**.

When Jesus was tempted in the wilderness (Matthew 4), He didn't argue or reason. He said:

"It is written…"

He used Scripture **strategically and vocally**. That's our pattern for victory.

Silent Battles and the First Time I Spoke Back

There was a season in my life when I was suffering from anxiety attacks almost daily. I read Scripture, but it stayed locked in my head—never spoken, never wielded. One day, in the middle of a breakdown, I finally said aloud:

"God has not given me a spirit of fear, but of power, love, and a sound mind."
— 2 Timothy 1:7

The atmosphere shifted. Not because the attack instantly ended, but because **I took authority with truth**. My silence broke—and so did the lie that I had no power.

That was the first time I understood: *Scripture becomes a sword when it's spoken.*

Supporting Scriptures to Strengthen Your Sword:

1. **Hebrews 4:12 (NIV)**

   "For the word of God is alive and active. Sharper than any double-edged sword..."

   The Word is not static—it slices through confusion, deception, and despair.

2. **Jeremiah 23:29 (ESV)**

   "Is not my word like fire, declares the Lord, and like a hammer that breaks the rock in pieces?"

   God's Word breaks through the hardest emotions and mental strongholds.

3. **Proverbs 18:21 (NLT)**

   "The tongue can bring death or life; those who love to talk will reap the consequences."

   What you speak either weakens or strengthens your spiritual battle posture.

Jesus in the Wilderness

In Matthew 4, Jesus was tired, hungry, and alone—emotionally and physically vulnerable.

Satan launched three temptations:

- To satisfy Himself outside of God's will
- To question God's faithfulness
- To manipulate Scripture for self-preservation

And every time, Jesus responded with:

"It is written..."

He wielded the Word **like a sword**. Not a whisper. Not a suggestion. A *rhema* word aimed precisely at the lie.

So must we.

⚔ Spiritual Warfare Teaching:
When to Swing the Sword

The sword is for:

- **Combatting lies** (e.g., "God doesn't love me" → *John 3:16*)
- **Rebuking fear** (e.g., "What if I fail?" → *Isaiah 41:10*)
- **Pushing back hopelessness** (e.g., "This will never change" → *Romans 8:28*)

But the sword is **useless** if it stays sheathed. Memorized truth must become *spoken truth*.

✒ How to Fight Back:

1. **Don't Just Read—Speak**
   God's Word isn't just for devotion—it's for battle. Silence

invites spiritual oppression. Speaking truth invites spiritual resistance.

2. **Write Your "Sword List"**

Create a list of go-to Scriptures for common emotional attacks:

- Fear → Isaiah 41:10
- Shame → Romans 8:1
- Hopelessness → Jeremiah 29:11
- Anxiety → Philippians 4:6–7

3. **Use Your Voice**

Jesus didn't think the Word—He declared it. Speak Scripture aloud every morning and whenever the attack comes.

4. **Declare "It Is Written" Statements**

Begin with those words:

"It is written…" and then finish it with a promise of God. Examples:

- "It is written: I will lie down and sleep in peace." – Psalm 4:8
- "It is written: No weapon formed against me shall prosper." – Isaiah 54:17
- "It is written: I have the mind of Christ." – 1 Corinthians 2:16

Faith in Action: "Draw Your Sword" Routine

Start practicing this each morning or during moments of attack:

1. **Identify the Lie**

   What anxious thought is attacking you?

2. **Find Your Verse**

   Ask the Holy Spirit to guide you to a Scripture that answers it.

3. **Speak It Aloud**

   "It is written…" followed by your chosen verse.

   Repeat. Boldly. Daily.

 Warfare Prayer

Lord,

Thank You for the power of Your Word. I confess that too often I've stayed silent while fear speaks loudly. Today, I take up the sword of the Spirit. Teach me to fight with Your truth. Let every lie fall at the sound of Your Word. Let every anxious thought be cut down with Your promises. May my mouth become a weapon of righteousness.

In Jesus' name, Amen.

 Scripture Declarations

❖ "It is written—God has not given me a spirit of fear."

- ❖ "God's Word is my weapon, my voice, and my peace."
- ❖ "The truth in my mouth will silence the chaos in my mind."

 Journal Prompt

What lie has been trying to live in your mind lately?

What Scripture can you begin to speak over it starting today?

Group Reflection Questions

1. Why is it important to speak Scripture aloud—not just think it?
2. Can you recall a time when a verse helped you push through panic or fear?
3. What "sword verse" will you begin carrying into battle with you this week?

CHAPTER 7
PRAYING IN
THE SPIRIT

Activating Peace Through Prayer

Primary Verse:

*"...praying at all times in the Spirit, with all prayer and
supplication."*

— Ephesians 6:18a (ESV)

Introduction: When Peace Requires More Than Words

There are times when prayer is easy—when the words flow and the atmosphere feels light. But there are also times when prayer feels like a struggle. When your mind is weary, your emotions are tangled, and words escape you.

That's when **praying in the Spirit** becomes essential.

Praying in the Spirit isn't about eloquence—it's about connection. It's the kind of prayer that rises from the depth of your soul and aligns your heart with God's presence, even when your thoughts are a mess. Whether it's through groans, quiet whispers, or even silent surrender, the Holy Spirit helps us intercede beyond what our minds can express.

In this chapter, we'll explore how Spirit-led prayer doesn't just bring peace—it **activates** it. When anxiety tries to lock you in silence, prayer unlocks power. When fear whispers lies, prayer speaks truth. This isn't about saying "perfect" prayers—it's about trusting the Spirit to carry you into God's peace, even in the storm.

Theological Insight:
Prayer Is the Power That Activates the Armor

After listing the six pieces of armor, Paul adds a seventh command—not a piece of armor per se, but the **spiritual power** that sustains them all: **prayer.**

The Greek phrase *"praying in the Spirit"* doesn't simply mean emotional praying or tongue-speaking (though it can include both); it means **Spirit-led, Spirit-directed, and Spirit-empowered communion with God.** It's prayer that flows from relationship, not routine.

Prayer is what **activates the armor**. Without it, you're dressed—but not dangerous. With it, you're not just protected— you're *empowered.*

✖ Common Lies We Often Live With:

- "I don't pray right—God won't listen to me."
- "If I don't feel it, my prayers don't count."
- "Prayer only works for spiritual people."
- "God's too busy to care about this."
- "I've prayed before, and nothing changed."

These lies try to keep you *silent, discouraged, and disconnected.* But prayer isn't about perfection—it's about **presence and partnership** with the Spirit of God.

When You Don't Know What to Say

Sometimes anxiety makes prayer feel impossible.

You try to pray, but your words feel blocked. You sit in silence, overwhelmed. Or maybe you're just numb, unsure what to even ask for.

I've been there—knees bent, heart racing, mind scattered.

That's when I learned: **You don't have to pray perfectly. You just have to pray.** The Holy Spirit meets you in the weakness and carries what you can't articulate.

"In the same way the Spirit helps us in our weakness. We do not know what we ought to pray for, but the Spirit Himself intercedes for us..."
— Romans 8:26 (NIV)

Your groans count. Your sighs count. Your whisper is heard.

The Prayer That Was Just a Whisper

I remember one night—after a long, anxious day—I curled up on the floor, not knowing what to say. I didn't have strength to "war in prayer." I just whispered, "Help."

That was it. One word.

And yet, I felt Him near. Not in thunder. Not in lightning. But in stillness. My breathing slowed. My thoughts quieted.

It reminded me: **God doesn't measure the length of your prayer. He honors the reach of your heart.**

 Supporting Scriptures for Spirit-Led Prayer:

1. **Romans 8:26–27 (NLT)**

   "The Holy Spirit helps us in our weakness... the Spirit pleads for us believers in harmony with God's own will."

Even when you don't know how to pray, the Spirit prays through you.

2. **Philippians 4:6–7 (NIV)**

   "Do not be anxious about anything, but in every situation, by prayer... present your requests to God. And the peace of God... will guard your hearts and minds..."

    Prayer is a peace-activator.

3. **Jude 1:20 (CSB)**

   "But you, dear friends, as you build yourselves up in your most holy faith, praying in the Holy Spirit..."

    Prayer strengthens you when anxiety weakens you.

Hannah — Pouring Out Her Soul

In 1 Samuel 1, Hannah was barren, broken, and deeply anxious. She had no children, no support, and an enemy who mocked her.

"In her deep anguish Hannah prayed to the Lord, weeping bitterly." — 1 Samuel 1:10

She wasn't polished. She didn't have fancy words. She just **poured out her soul** before the Lord.

And the result?

"Her face was no longer downcast." — 1 Samuel 1:18

Her situation hadn't changed yet. But prayer shifted her **perspective**, **posture**, and **peace.**

✕ Spiritual Warfare Teaching:
Prayer Breaks the Cycle

The enemy loves to use anxiety to create a loop:

1. You feel anxious
2. You don't pray
3. You feel worse
4. You isolate
5. Anxiety grows

But Spirit-led prayer **breaks the cycle.**

- It refocuses your thoughts
- Reorients your emotions
- Replaces lies with truth
- Reconnects you to God's presence

🔫 How to Fight Back:

1. **Let Go of Prayer Performance**
   You don't need the perfect words—just honest ones. The Holy Spirit fills in the gaps.

2. **Make Prayer Your First Response, Not Your Last Resort**

Don't wait until you're falling apart to pray. Let prayer *prepare* your heart before the attack.

3. **Use "Breathe Prayers"**
   When anxiety hits, inhale and pray silently:
   Inhale: "You are near…"
   Exhale: "…and I am not alone."

4. **Set Alarms for Prayer Pauses**
   Schedule a moment to pause at 10am, 2pm, or before bed to say a one-line prayer or just invite the Holy Spirit.

🔒 Bonus: Praying Scripture Aloud

- Here are examples of turning Scripture into spoken prayers:

- "Lord, guard my heart and mind with Your peace." (Phil. 4:7)

- "Spirit of God, intercede when I can't find the words." (Rom. 8:26)

- "I build myself up in faith by praying in the Spirit." (Jude 1:20)

Prayer isn't just defensive—it's how you stay connected to **the Commander of your peace.**

Faith in Action: "Prayer Pulse" Strategy

Start praying in the Spirit throughout your day by following this rhythm:

- **Morning:** "Lord, I give this day to You. Lead me by Your Spirit."
- **Midday:** "Holy Spirit, help me stay grounded in peace."
- **Evening:** "God, guard my mind tonight. Speak truth in my rest."

You don't need long, poetic prayers. Just real ones.

 Warfare Prayer

Holy Spirit,

Thank You for being my helper, advocate, and intercessor. When my words fail, You speak for me. When my thoughts race, You calm me. I invite You to lead my prayers. Help me to pray beyond my emotions—into truth, strength, and alignment with God's will. Fill my room, my car, my heart with Your presence. Teach me to pray in power.
In Jesus' name, Amen.

 Scripture Declarations
- ❖ "I will pray in the Spirit and not grow weary."
- ❖ "When I don't know what to say, God still hears me."
- ❖ "Peace rises when I pray—anxiety flees when I speak."

Journal Prompt

When is prayer hardest for you, and why?

How can you invite the Holy Spirit to pray through you more freely?

Group Reflection Questions

1. What does "praying in the Spirit" mean to you practically?
2. Have you ever experienced peace after a prayer—even when your problem remained?
3. What would happen if you turned your anxious thoughts into spontaneous prayers?

CHAPTER 8

AFTER THE
BATTLE

Living in Victory, Not in Fear of the
Next Attack

Primary Verse:

"Now thanks be to God who always leads us in triumph in
Christ..." — 2 Corinthians 2:14 (NKJV)

Introduction: The War Is Real—But So Is the Victory

When you've been through anxiety, fear, and spiritual warfare, even after the worst of it passes... something still lingers:

- *What if it comes back?*
- *What if I'm not strong enough next time?*
- *What if this peace is temporary?*

This is the **post-battle fear**—the shadow that creeps in after the storm has quieted.

But here's the truth: **God doesn't just deliver you from the battle—He equips you to live in peace afterward.** The victory isn't fragile—it's **founded in Christ**. And His triumph is not a moment; it's a mindset.

⚚ Theological Insight:

Victory Is a Walk, Not Just a Win

Paul writes in 2 Corinthians 2:14 that God *"leads us in triumph."* The word here implies **a continual procession**—like a Roman general leading his army in a victory parade. The battle is over, and **the walk of triumph has begun.**

But many of us don't walk like victors. We walk like survivors. Guarded. Waiting for the next hit. Constantly on edge.

Living in victory doesn't mean you'll never feel fear again. It means you **refuse to live under its rule.**

✖ Common Lies We Often Live With:

- "The peace won't last."
- "I have to stay alert or the enemy will get me again."
- "If I let my guard down, I'll fall apart."
- "I'm not strong enough to maintain this victory."
- "One mistake and I'll be right back where I started."

These lies turn **triumph into tension**—keeping us bound by fear even after the fight is over.

I Didn't Know How to Relax Anymore

After a long season of anxiety, I reached a place of breakthrough. My body calmed. My thoughts settled. My soul finally *exhaled*.

But strangely, I didn't feel safe. I felt... uneasy. I kept checking the "emotional horizon" for another wave. I realized I'd been so used to *fighting* that I didn't know how to *rest*.

That's when God gently reminded me:

"The Lord will fight for you; you need only to be still." — Exodus 14:14

I wasn't meant to stay in combat mode. I was called to walk in confidence.

When Rest Felt Risky

There was a time when I couldn't enjoy peace. I'd survived such intense anxiety that even quiet moments made me nervous. I was *waiting for the next shoe to drop*. I kept rehearsing "what if" scenarios in my head.

It wasn't that I didn't trust God. I didn't trust the *pause*. I'd confused constant awareness with spiritual maturity. But God showed me that **rest isn't weakness—it's worship**. It's trusting Him enough to stop bracing for battle and start embracing His presence.

 Supporting Scriptures to Live in Victory:

1. **Romans 8:37 (NIV)**

   "In all these things we are more than conquerors through Him who loved us."

    Victory isn't just surviving—it's overcoming.

2. **Isaiah 26:3 (ESV)**

   "You keep him in perfect peace whose mind is stayed on You..."

    Peace is maintained through focus—not fear.

3. **Psalm 18:39 (CSB)**

"You have clothed me with strength for battle; You subdue my adversaries beneath me."

 God doesn't just protect you—He empowers you.

Joshua After Jericho

Jericho was a miraculous victory. The walls fell. Israel conquered. But after the victory came a new challenge: **How do we keep walking in obedience without falling into fear?**

God told Joshua repeatedly:

"Be strong and courageous… Do not be afraid." (Joshua 1:9)

Victory wasn't just about one city—it was about establishing a **lifestyle of faith**.

The same applies to you.

⚔ Spiritual Warfare Teaching:
Winning Is a Lifestyle

To live in victory after the battle, you must:

1. **Stay armored** — Just because the fire has stopped doesn't mean the battle is over.

2. **Renew your routines** — Shift from *defensive survival* to *active peacebuilding*.

3. **Keep worship close** — Praise is not just for emergencies—it's for everyday living.

How to Fight Back:

1. **Rehearse God's Faithfulness**

   Don't just relive the trauma—relive the *testimony*. Keep a "victory journal" where you list past breakthroughs.

2. **Identify Your Triggers**

   Are there certain thoughts or sounds that spike your tension again? Don't ignore them—name them and reframe them with truth.

3. **Practice Rest as Resistance**

   Set aside 15 minutes of stillness each day. Not to "do" something—but to "be" in God's presence. Stillness is spiritual warfare too.

4. **Reset Your Identity**

   Instead of calling yourself a "survivor," begin calling yourself a *conqueror*.

Bonus: Living from a Victory Mindset

- When fear says, "What if it happens again?"

  → Declare: "Even if it does, God will meet me there too."

- When anxiety whispers, "You're still broken..."

  → Declare: "I am healed, restored, and walking whole."

- When your past tries to define your now...

    → Declare: "I am led in **triumph** by Christ—not in torment by memory."

Faith in Action: Victory Walk Plan

1. Morning: Declare this: *"I am not afraid of the future—I walk in triumph."*

> a. Speak out: "Victory is my new normal. I don't live in survival mode anymore."
>
> b. Stretch and breathe deeply—rest in the presence of the Holy Spirit.

2. Midday: Pause to thank God for where He's brought you from.

> a. Listen to a worship song that declares victory.
>
> b. Write down one lie that tried to come up— and a verse that shuts it down.

3. Evening: Reflect: *Where did I walk in peace today? Where did fear try to creep back in?*

> a. Journal where you noticed peace and thank God for it.
>
> b. Pray a short prayer of release: "Lord, I won't carry old battles into tomorrow."

Warfare Prayer

God of Victory,

You are the God who fights for me—but also the God who walks with me after the battle. I declare that I am not stuck in survival. I am stepping into rest, peace, and daily confidence. Silence every voice of fear that tries to creep back in. Teach me how to live like a conqueror, not just a fighter. My victory is not a one-time event—it's a lifestyle of walking in Your strength. In Jesus' name, Amen.

 Scripture Declarations

- "I walk in peace, not paranoia."
- "I am more than a conqueror."
- "My life is not defined by fear, but by faith in Christ."
- "My peace is permanent—not passing."
- I have rest on every side because the Lord gives it."
- "Victory is not just behind me—it's beneath me and before me.

 Journal Prompt

Are you still mentally fighting battles that have already been won? What would living in victory *look like* for you this week?

Group Reflection Questions

1. Why is it sometimes harder to rest after a battle than to fight in one?
2. What habits can help you live in victory instead of emotional vigilance?
3. What victory has God already given you that you need to *fully receive*?

CHAPTER 9

THE VOICE
BEHIND THE FEAR

Discerning the Enemy's Whisper

Primary Verse:

"My sheep hear My voice, and I know them, and they follow Me. A stranger they will not follow, but they will flee from him."

— John 10:27, 5 (ESV)

Introduction: Not Every Voice Deserves Your Attention

Fear speaks. Sometimes loudly. Sometimes subtly.
It sounds like:

- *"This is going to fall apart."*
- *"You always mess things up."*
- *"God has forgotten you."*

But behind every recurring fear, there's often a **spiritual source**—an enemy voice whispering with **strategic intent**. Satan rarely attacks with volume; he attacks with **suggestion**.

Just like in the Garden of Eden, the enemy still says:
"Did God really say...?"

Anxiety often stems from **listening to the wrong voice**—and taking it as truth.

⚜ Theological Insight:
The Enemy Is a Liar and a Mimic

Jesus called Satan the "father of lies" (John 8:44). He speaks *not from truth* but from **twisted distortion**. He uses half-truths, past wounds, emotional weak points, and fears to **create confusion**.

He doesn't always sound evil. Sometimes he sounds **logical**. Reasonable. Even *like you*.

But if the voice leads to fear, shame, paralysis, or accusation—it's not God.

"For God has not given us a spirit of fear…" — 2 Timothy 1:7

✖ Common Lies We Often Live With:

- "You're not really saved."
- "This peace won't last."
- "God is disappointed in you."
- "You're not strong enough."
- "Everyone else is doing better than you."
- "If God loved you, you wouldn't feel like this."

These lies are not just internal doubts—they are spiritual whispers meant to shake your identity and steal your peace.

A Voice That Wasn't My Own

I remember driving home late one night when a random, discouraging thought hit me like a wave:

"You're doing all this for nothing. It's never going to change."

At first, I thought it was just me being tired. But it was more than that—it felt spiritual. It came with *weight.* And it came **suddenly**, like a dart.

I pulled over and spoke this verse out loud:

"I demolish arguments and every pretension that sets itself up against the knowledge of God..." — 2 Corinthians 10:5.

Instantly, clarity came. It wasn't my voice. It wasn't God's voice. It was an attack—and I shut it down.

When Lies Dress Like Truth

During a particularly heavy season, I found myself stuck in a loop of self-doubt. After praying and journaling, I wrote, *"Maybe I'm too broken to be used by God."* It felt like a conclusion—but it was really an attack in disguise.

A mentor asked me, "Would Jesus ever say that to you?"

The answer was clear: *No.* That voice was not my Shepherd's. It was an impostor with a counterfeit message.

 Supporting Scriptures to Help You Discern Voices:

1. **John 10:4–5 (NIV)**

   "His sheep follow Him because they know His voice... They will never follow a stranger..."

   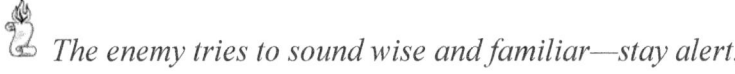 *God's voice leads to peace, even in challenge. The enemy's voice leads to torment.*

2. **2 Corinthians 11:14 (ESV)**

   "Satan disguises himself as an angel of light."

   The enemy tries to sound wise and familiar—stay alert.

3. **1 John 4:1 (CSB)**

    "Test the spirits to see if they are from God."

    Every voice must be tested against the Word and the peace of God.

Jesus and Peter

In Matthew 16, Peter tells Jesus, *"You will never suffer or die."*

Jesus responds not with thanks—but with rebuke:
"Get behind Me, Satan!" (v.23)

Peter meant well. But the **source** of the statement was not God. Jesus discerned the voice **behind** the moment—and shut it down.

We must do the same with thoughts that sound kind but contradict truth.

✕ Spiritual Warfare Teaching:
How to Test the Voice

Ask yourself:

- Does this voice lead to peace or fear?
- Does it align with Scripture or twist it?
- Does it strengthen my faith or drain it?
- Does it reflect the character of Christ?

If the answer is fear, shame, or confusion—**it must be silenced.**

🖊 How to Fight Back:

1. **Speak truth out loud** — Use the Word like Jesus did: "It is written…"

2. **Memorize go-to verses** — Especially those that affirm identity (e.g., Romans 8:1, John 1:12, 2 Tim. 1:7).

3. **Worship through the whisper** — Praise silences the enemy.

4. **Ask the Holy Spirit to confirm truth** — God is not the author of confusion (1 Cor. 14:33).

5. **Surround yourself with truth-tellers** — Let godly community speak what's real when your own thoughts feel foggy.

Faith in Action: The "Voice Test" Strategy

Write this in your journal or phone:

1. **The Thought:**
   What did I hear in my mind or heart?

2. **The Emotion:**
   What feeling did it bring? (peace, fear, shame, pressure)

3. **The Source:**

Compare it to Scripture. Would Jesus say this to you?

4. **The Response:**

Rebuke it or receive it. Speak truth over it.

 Warfare Prayer

Jesus,

I want to know Your voice. Teach me to discern between truth and subtle deception. Silence the enemy's whisper in my mind. I renounce every false word, every lie, every fear-based thought that didn't come from You. Speak louder, Lord. Tune my spirit to hear the Shepherd and flee from the stranger.

In Jesus' name, Amen.

 Scripture Declarations

❖ "I know the voice of my Shepherd—I will not follow another."

❖ "I test every thought with truth."

❖ I will not partner with fear, shame, or lies

❖ "Fear does not lead me—faith does."

❖ God's truth is louder than anxiety's whisper

Journal Prompt

What voice have you been listening to that might not be God's?
What would God say about the same situation?

What's one fearful thought or phrase you've believed that did not come from God?
What truth from Scripture speaks directly against it?

Group Reflection Questions

1. Why is it easy to confuse your own thoughts with the enemy's whisper?
2. What's one fear-based thought that seemed harmless—but actually carried spiritual weight?
3. How can you develop a habit of testing every voice by the Word of God?
4. How can we tell when fear is spiritual and not just emotional?

CHAPTER 10

THE ARMOR IN THE MIDNIGHT HOUR

Fighting Anxiety When the World is Quiet

Key Verse:

"At midnight I rise to give you thanks for your righteous laws."

— Psalm 119:62 (NIV)

Introduction: When the Night Feels Like a Battle

It's one thing to feel anxious during the day—when life is moving, people are present, and distractions are everywhere. But **nighttime anxiety** is different. The world is quiet, but your thoughts are loud. Stillness surrounds you, but your soul is stirring. The darkness outside seems to reflect the unease within.

That's because the enemy often intensifies his attacks when your defenses are low and **your mind is still**.

The **midnight hour** is both literal and spiritual. It represents those moments when:

- You feel alone and unseen
- You replay your regrets
- You fear the unknown
- You question everything in silence

But the good news? **God does some of His best work at midnight.**

 Theological Insight:

Midnight Warfare in Scripture

1. **Paul and Silas in Prison (Acts 16:25–26)**

    "About midnight Paul and Silas were praying and singing hymns to God... and suddenly there was a violent earthquake..."

They didn't wait for the morning—they worshiped in the midnight.

2. **Psalm 119:62**

   "At midnight I rise to give you thanks for your righteous laws."

    David practiced praise when others slept.

3. **Exodus 12:29**

   "At midnight the Lord struck down all the firstborn in Egypt..."

    God's deliverance came in the darkest hour.

These verses show us a pattern: **Midnight isn't just a time of trial—it's a doorway for breakthrough.**

✖ Common Lies We Often Live With:

- "Everyone else is sleeping peacefully—something must be wrong with me."
- "If I can't sleep, I'll be exhausted and fail tomorrow."
- "Nighttime is when the worst thoughts are true."
- "God feels distant in the dark."
- "The silence means I'm alone."

These lies thrive in the quiet, but they are dismantled by the Word. The enemy wants the night to feel like isolation, but God is never asleep—and neither is His love or protection.

My Battle at 2:00 AM

There was a season when I dreaded going to sleep. Not because I feared nightmares—but because I feared **my own thoughts.**

I'd lie awake with:

- "What if tomorrow's too much?"
- "Did I handle that conversation wrong?"
- "Why do I feel like I'm failing?"

It was hard to rest when my mind wouldn't. Until I began using **midnight as ministry**—not just misery.

One night, I got up, opened Psalm 91, and prayed it aloud. I felt nothing at first. But I kept going. Line by line. Word by word.

Peace didn't come instantly—but it came.

When The Dark Felt Loud

At first, I used to joke about it—how I became a "nighttime overthinker." But when the laughter faded, I had to admit the truth.

Night was when everything got loud.
The fear.
The regrets.

The sense that I was one bad thought away from completely falling apart.

I'd lie in bed, staring at the ceiling while my mind raced. The silence in the room only made the noise inside me worse. I'd open every app on my phone, hoping to drown it out—but it never helped. I still felt like I was sinking beneath the weight of my own thoughts.

Then one evening, after a day that had drained everything from me, I reached for something different. I don't even know why, but instead of opening social media, I opened my Bible app. The verse of the day was Psalm 27. I read it out loud—twice.

"The Lord is my light and my salvation—whom shall I fear?"

That night didn't erase the anxiety. But it shifted something deep inside me. I lit a candle. Turned on soft worship music. And read those words like medicine for my soul.

It wasn't magic. But for the first time in a long time, I didn't feel completely alone in the dark.

That choice—to reach for God instead of distraction—became my quiet rebellion. My first real step toward peace.

Supporting Scriptures to Help You Discern Voices:

1. **John 10:27** – "My sheep hear My voice, and I know them, and they follow Me."

   o *God's voice leads to peace, not panic.*

2. **2 Corinthians 10:5** – "We demolish arguments and every pretension… and we take captive every thought to make it obedient to Christ."

   o *Every voice must be brought under the authority of the Word.*

3. **1 John 4:1** – "Beloved, do not believe every spirit, but test the spirits to see whether they are from God..."

   o *Just because it's loud doesn't mean it's true.*

4. **Romans 8:16** – "The Spirit himself bears witness with our spirit that we are children of God."

   o *God's voice confirms identity, not shame.*

Gideon — Called in the Midnight Hour

Scripture Reference: Judges 6:11–27

Gideon didn't look like a warrior. He felt like a failure. When we meet him, he's hiding in a winepress, threshing wheat in fear of his enemies. But God saw something different. He called Gideon "mighty warrior"—while he was still trembling in the dark.

Midnight Fear Moment

Gideon wrestled with fear at night—literally. When God instructed him to tear down his father's altar to Baal and replace it with one for the Lord, **Gideon did it at night** out of fear (Judges 6:27). He obeyed, but in the shadows. God didn't scold him—He worked with his weakness.

What We Learn:

- God doesn't wait until we feel brave to use us.
- Obedience in the dark is still obedience.
- God calls us who we *are becoming*, not just who we *feel like* in the moment.

Application for Your Midnight Hour

You may feel like Gideon—uncertain, unqualified, and overwhelmed. But the same God who showed up in Gideon's fear will meet you in yours. Even if you can't roar, whisper your *yes*. Even in the middle of the night, God's calling still stands.

"God sees mighty warriors even in trembling hearts."

 ### How to Wear the Armor at Night

1. Helmet of Salvation

→ Speak this aloud: *"My mind is covered. I am saved, secure, and sealed."*

2. **Breastplate of Righteousness**

   → Remind yourself: *"My value isn't in how I feel but who I am in Christ."*

3. **Belt of Truth**

   → Declare: *"Anxious thoughts are not facts. God's Word is final."*

4. **Shoes of Peace**

   → Put both feet on the floor and pray: *"I stand in peace tonight, not panic."*

5. **Shield of Faith**

   → Whisper verses out loud. Each one is a shield blocking fiery darts.

6. **Sword of the Spirit**

   → Read a psalm. Speak a promise. Slice through silence with Scripture.

7. **Prayer in the Spirit**

   → Let your groans, whispers, or even tears become your intercession.

⚔ Spiritual Warfare Teaching:
How to Test the Voice

Not every thought that enters your mind is from you—or from God. The enemy is a master of impersonation. He plants *suggestions* that sound like *self-condemnation*:

- "You'll never change."
- "God is disappointed in you."
- "You should've known better."

But God doesn't guilt-trip His children. His voice corrects with love, not cruelty.

Here's how to test the voice:

1. Does it align with Scripture?
2. Does it lead you closer to God or deeper into fear?
3. Does it sound like condemnation or conviction?
4. Does it bring confusion—or clarity in Christ?

When in doubt, go back to what's written. If the voice contradicts the Word, *it's not your Shepherd.*

🗡 **How to Fight Back:**

- **Set a "midnight plan" ahead of time.** Choose your worship playlist, favorite psalm, and a comfortable space in advance.

- **Keep a verse by your bedside.** Example: *"In peace I will lie down and sleep, for you alone, Lord, make me dwell in safety."* (Psalm 4:8)

- **Turn your bed into a battlefield—but not with fear. With faith.**

- **Remember that praise is warfare.** You don't have to feel strong to worship—you just have to show up.
- **Call anxiety what it is: a nighttime intruder.** But God is the watchman of your soul.

Faith in Action: The "Voice Test" Strategy

- **Step 1: Capture the thought.**
  Write down exactly what you heard in your mind (ex: "I'll never be free from this.")

- **Step 2: Compare it to truth.**
  Ask: "Does this line up with what God says?"

- **Step 3: Declare God's Word instead.**
  Replace the lie with Scripture (ex: "Whom the Son sets free is free indeed." — John 8:36)

- **Step 4: Speak it out loud.**
  You fight spirit with spirit. Use the Sword of the Spirit—*the Word of God spoken aloud.*

Midnight Worship Plan

Try this when anxiety visits you at night:

- Play soft worship music
- Light a candle or open your Bible app to Psalms
- Read Psalm 91, 27, or 42 out loud
- Journal one sentence of thanks:
- "God, even here in the dark, You are near."

Midnight Prayer

Father,

The night feels long and lonely sometimes. But You are the God of midnight. You see me in the shadows. You hold me in the silence. I put on Your armor now—not just for the morning, but for this moment. Cover my mind. Calm my heart. Speak peace into this room. I invite Your presence into the quiet places of my soul. Let me sleep in safety and rise in strength.

In Jesus' name, Amen.

 Scripture Declarations

Declare these out loud when the voices of fear, shame, or confusion try to rise:

- ❖ "I hear my Shepherd's voice, and I follow Him." — John 10:27
- ❖ "No weapon formed against my mind will prosper." — Isaiah 54:17
- ❖ "God's Spirit leads me into truth, not torment." — John 16:13
- ❖ "I take every thought captive and make it obey Christ." — 2 Corinthians 10:5
- ❖ "I will not be led by fear—I am led by peace." — Colossians 3:15

 **Journal Prompt**

What anxious thoughts tend to surface at night for you?
What verse can you begin using as your "midnight sword"?

Group Reflection Questions

1. Why do you think anxiety often intensifies at night?

2. How can we turn the midnight hour into a moment of intimacy with God?

3. Share a time when God met you in your darkest hour— literally or spiritually.

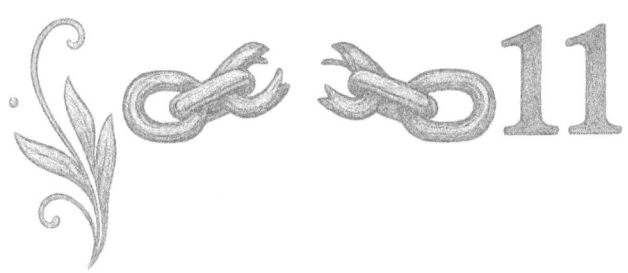

CHAPTER 11

BREAKING THE CYCLE

Generational Anxiety and Spiritual
Patterns

Primary Verse:

*"Christ redeemed us from the curse of the law by becoming a
curse for us..."*

— Galatians 3:13 (ESV)

Introduction: When You Inherit More Than DNA

Some battles we fight aren't just *ours*—they're *inherited*.

Anxiety, fear, and emotional instability can run in families—not just biologically, but spiritually and behaviorally. You may have grown up hearing things like:

- *"We've always been worriers."*
- *"It's just how our family is."*
- *"Don't expect peace—just survive."*

But what seems *normal* in your lineage may actually be a **cycle that needs to be broken.**

The good news? Through Christ, you don't have to live in what you were raised in. **You are adopted into a new spiritual family**—one marked by faith, not fear.

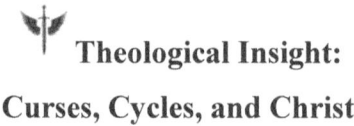

Theological Insight:
Curses, Cycles, and Christ

Scripture teaches about **patterns of sin and struggle** being passed down generationally (Exodus 20:5). But Jesus came to **redeem us from every curse** and to give us access to a **new inheritance** (Galatians 3:13–14).

This means:

- You don't have to carry what your parents or grandparents carried.

- Anxiety may be familiar—but it isn't *final*.

- You can walk in freedom, even if it wasn't modeled for you.

❌ Common Lies We Often Live With:

- "This is just how our family is—we're always anxious."
- "If they couldn't break free, neither can I."
- "It's in my blood—there's no point in trying to change."
- "Peace is for other people, not me."
- "Some families are chosen for blessing… mine was built for burden."

These lies chain us to a legacy that Christ already broke on the cross.

My Anxiety Wasn't Just Mine

For years I dealt with racing thoughts, emotional shutdowns, and performance-driven fear. But the more I examined my family history, I realized something:

Everyone in my family coped this way.

We didn't talk about emotions. We stuffed them. We overworked, overthought, and overcontrolled.

It wasn't just *me*—it was a **generational pattern**.

Once I named it, I was able to break it. Through prayer, Scripture, and surrender—I rewrote the pattern. And by God's grace, I'm walking a new path for the next generation.

The Moment I Saw the Cycle

I remember sitting with an older relative as they nervously tapped their foot, sighing over a problem that hadn't even happened yet. It reminded me of my own pattern—assuming the worst, bracing for disaster, living in hypervigilance.

It was in that moment I realized: *This didn't start with me. But it can stop with me.*

My anxiety had a history. But I also had a **Helper**—the Holy Spirit—who could rewrite my future.

 Supporting Scriptures for Breaking Cycles:

1. **Galatians 3:13–14 (NIV)**

   "Christ redeemed us from the curse... that the blessing given to Abraham might come to the Gentiles..."

   🕊 *You don't inherit curses—you inherit blessing in Christ.*

2. **Ezekiel 18:20 (ESV)**

   "The son shall not suffer for the iniquity of the father..."

God holds each generation responsible for their own choices—cycles can stop with you.

3. **Romans 8:15 (CSB)**

   "You did not receive a spirit of slavery to fall back into fear, but you received the Spirit of adoption…"

You don't have to repeat cycles—you are adopted into freedom.

Abraham → Isaac → Jacob

Each of these men had moments of faith—but also cycles of **fear and deception**:

- Abraham lied to protect himself.
- Isaac repeated the same lie.
- Jacob became known for manipulation.

The pattern intensified—until Jacob wrestled with God and **was renamed Israel.**

Sometimes **a generational breakthrough begins with a personal wrestling.**

Spiritual Warfare Teaching:
Renouncing and Rewriting the Pattern

To break generational anxiety or spiritual cycles:

1. **Identify the Pattern**

   What fear, behavior, or belief is recurring across generations?

2. **Renounce the Agreement**

   Speak: *"I break every agreement I've made with fear, shame, or silence."*

3. **Declare Your New Lineage**

   You are in the family of Christ. Your spiritual DNA is rewired.

4. **Establish New Rhythms**

   Begin replacing inherited habits with holy ones.

How to Fight Back:

1. **Name the Pattern.**

   Look at your family history honestly—not to blame, but to gain clarity. Identify repeated behaviors or beliefs tied to fear.

2. **Break Agreement with the Lie.**

   Say out loud: *"In Jesus' name, I no longer agree with the lie that this cycle defines me."*

3. **Replace with Truth.**

   Declare Galatians 3:13: *"Christ redeemed me from every curse. I am not bound—I am blessed."*

4. **Pray Over Future Generations.**
   Begin to speak blessings, freedom, and emotional healing over your children, siblings, or nieces and nephews. What starts with you can free them too.

5. **Walk Differently.**
   Build new habits of honesty, peace, rest, and trust. Make your life a testimony of what God can rewrite.

Faith in Action: Family Freedom Declaration

Write and speak this:

"In the name of Jesus, I break every cycle of anxiety, fear, emotional avoidance, and inner torment in my bloodline. I declare that I walk in peace, purpose, and truth. I inherit the blessings of the Lord, and I pass down victory to the generations after me."

 Warfare Prayer

Father,

I bring my family history before You—not in shame, but in surrender. Where anxiety has ruled generations before me, let peace now reign. Where emotional brokenness has been handed down, I receive healing and wholeness. Thank You for making me new in Christ. Break every cycle that has held me back. Let my freedom mark a new path for those who come after me.
In Jesus' name, Amen.

Scripture Declarations

- ❖ "I am not bound by generational fear—I walk in spiritual freedom."
- ❖ "I am a chain-breaker, not a carrier."
- ❖ "What started in my family ends in me—through Christ, I begin a new story."

 Journal Prompt

What patterns of fear, control, or anxiety have existed in your family?

What would it look like for you to walk in the opposite spirit?

Group Reflection Questions

1. How can emotional or spiritual patterns be unintentionally passed down?

2. What specific "generational" habits are you now choosing to break?

3. What family messages have you carried that God never spoke?

CHAPTER 12

FROM ANXIOUS
TO ANCHORED

Establishing New Rhythms of Rest and
Renewal

Primary Verse:

"This hope we have as an anchor for the soul, firm and secure."

— Hebrews 6:19 (CSB)

Introduction: When You've Lived in Survival Mode Too Long

Anxiety makes you reactive. You brace for the worst. You micromanage your thoughts, your schedule, your emotions—until exhaustion feels normal.

But freedom from anxiety doesn't mean *just not panicking.* It means learning to **live anchored.**

God doesn't want us constantly fluctuating between peace and panic. He wants us **rooted** in daily rhythms of **rest, renewal, and relationship with Him.**

"Be still and know that I am God..." — Psalm 46:10

Stillness is not laziness. It's spiritual **anchoring.**

⚜ Theological Insight:
Anchor Your Soul, Not Just Your Day

Hebrews 6:19 describes hope in Christ as an **anchor for the soul**—not for the schedule, not for the to-do list, not even for the feelings, but for the **soul.**

That means when emotions rise, circumstances change, or thoughts swirl, your soul can still be **anchored in hope.**

This hope isn't optimism—it's **confidence in the unchanging character of God.**

✖ Common Lies We Often Live With:

- "If I stop moving, everything will fall apart."
- "Rest is for the weak or lazy."
- "I don't have time to slow down."
- "God only helps those who stay busy."
- "Stillness is unsafe—it's when the worry creeps in."

⚠ *These lies confuse productivity with peace—and wear us down spiritually.*

I Didn't Know How to Rest

After a long season of spiritual warfare and anxiety, I realized something: I didn't know how to be still.

If I wasn't worrying, I was working. If I wasn't doing something, I felt unproductive—and therefore unsafe.

Rest felt irresponsible.

But then I read:

"In returning and rest you shall be saved; in quietness and trust shall be your strength." — Isaiah 30:15 (ESV)

God was calling me not just to peace—but to **practice it.**

The Illusion of Control

There was a season where I couldn't sit in silence for more than a few minutes. I felt like I had to be doing something—fixing something—otherwise anxiety would crawl back in.

But the constant motion was masking a deeper fear: *I didn't trust that I was held when I wasn't in control.*

Only when I began scheduling moments of stillness—reading Scripture with my coffee instead of scrolling, breathing deeply before answering texts, going to sleep without noise—did I begin to experience what it meant to be anchored.

Not just calmed. Anchored.

 Supporting Scriptures for Anchoring Your Life:

1. **Hebrews 6:19 (CSB)**

   "We have this hope as an anchor for the soul, firm and secure."

    Hope is not a wish—it's a weight that keeps you grounded.

2. **Matthew 11:28–29 (NLT)**

   "Come to me, all of you who are weary... and I will give you rest."

   Rest is found in presence, not performance.

3. **Isaiah 58:11 (NIV)**

   "The Lord will guide you always... You will be like a well-watered garden."

God's rhythm brings restoration—not burnout.

Mary of Bethany

In Luke 10:38–42, while Martha was anxious and busy, Mary **sat** at Jesus' feet. She wasn't lazy—she was **anchored**.

Jesus said:

"Mary has chosen what is better, and it will not be taken away from her."

Sometimes anxiety masquerades as "being responsible." But peace isn't passive—it's **intentional positioning**.

⚔ Spiritual Warfare Teaching:

Anxiety Breaks Rhythm—God Restores It

The enemy loves to keep you:

- Busy but empty
- Productive but panicked
- Awake but unrested

One of your greatest weapons against anxiety is **establishing holy rhythm.** That includes:

- **Sabbath rest**
- **Morning Scripture reading**
- **Regular gratitude journaling**
- **Evening reflection without screens**

How to Fight Back:

1. **Schedule Stillness.**
   If you don't make time for peace, anxiety will steal your time with panic. Block moments of silence with Godlike appointments.

2. **Anchor in Truth.**
   Speak Hebrews 6:19 aloud: *"My soul is anchored in the hope of Christ. I will not drift with fear."*

3. **Replace Hurry with Holiness.**
   Turn busyness into intentionality. Ask: *"Am I doing this from rest—or from fear?"*

4. **Practice Presence.**
   Take a deep breath, invite the Holy Spirit in, and remind yourself: *"I am safe. I am seen. I am still."*

Faith in Action: Anchoring Habits to Start This Week

1. **Sacred Mornings:**
   Start your day with 10 minutes of Scripture before social media or email.

2. **Midday Reset:**
   Pause for 2–3 minutes of deep breathing + speak one verse aloud.

3. **Evening Wind-Down:**
   Write one gratitude moment + read a Psalm before bed.

Start small. Repeat often. Stay anchored.

 Warfare Prayer

Lord, Anchor of My Soul,

I confess that I've let anxiety set the rhythm of my life. I rush, worry, and rarely stop to breathe. But You call me to rest. You call me to stillness. Anchor my soul in You. Help me build rhythms of worship, rest, and renewal that restore what fear has drained. Teach me that peace is not a break—it's my inheritance. In Jesus' name, Amen.

 Scripture Declarations

- ❖ "My soul is anchored in hope."
- ❖ "I build my day on God's rhythm, not on anxiety."
- ❖ "Stillness is my strength. Peace is my path."
- ❖ "I trade exhaustion for rest."
- ❖ My peace is not fragile—it is anchored in Christ.
- ❖ I live from a rhythm of grace, not performance.
- ❖ My rest is warfare, and my stillness is strength.

 Journal Prompt

What part of your daily rhythm feels most chaotic or unanchored? What's one small, daily habit you can begin that invites peace?

Group Reflection Questions

1. Why is stillness so difficult for anxious people?
2. How can healthy routines serve as spiritual warfare tools?
3. Why is it hard to rest in a busy, anxious world?

CHAPTER 13

THE ANOINTED MIND

Renewing Thought Patterns Through
the Spirit

Primary Verse:

*"Do not be conformed to this world, but be transformed by the
renewing of your mind..."*

— Romans 12:2 (ESV)

Introduction: When Your Thoughts Become Your Traps

Anxiety doesn't usually begin with a crisis—it begins with a **thought**.

- *"What if I can't handle this?"*
- *"I'm probably going to fail again."*
- *"Something bad always happens eventually."*

Over time, thoughts become pathways—then highways. Eventually, they become **strongholds**. But God doesn't just want to stop your thoughts. He wants to **anoint your mind** and **renew your patterns**.

Theological Insight:

Your Mind Was Made for Truth

Romans 12:2 calls us to **transformation through renewal**. The Greek word for "renewing" (*anakainōsis*) means "complete renovation."

This is not self-help. This is **Spirit-empowered reconstruction** of the mind.

Through Christ, you don't just try harder to stop anxious thoughts—you submit them to the **Holy Spirit**, who rebuilds your patterns from the inside out.

"We have the mind of Christ." — 1 Corinthians 2:16.

This means your thought life is no longer governed by fear, shame, or self-sabotage. It's governed by truth, clarity, and peace.

✖ Common Lies We Often Live With:

- "I can't help how I think—it's just how my brain works."
- "If I don't worry about it, I won't be prepared."
- "God is disappointed with my thought life."
- "Peace is for people who don't have my past."
- "It's impossible to stop these spirals—I'll never have a sound mind."

⚠ *These lies keep you chained to cycles Christ already broke.*

My Mind Needed Healing

There were seasons in my life when I could preach peace to others—but couldn't find it in my own mind.

I'd spiral into worst-case thinking. I'd overanalyze conversations for hours. I'd replay regret on loop like a broken record.

It wasn't until I stopped trying to "think better" and started **praying over my mind** that I experienced true change. The shift happened when I said:

"Holy Spirit, anoint my thought life. Rewire what anxiety built."

When Fear Woke Up First

I remember a morning when I woke up already overwhelmed. Nothing had gone wrong yet—but my thoughts were racing, my stomach was tight, and I felt spiritually foggy.

I hadn't spoken a word, but I'd already had 20 conversations—in my head. All negative. All based in fear.

That day, I made a choice: I sat still and said out loud, *"Holy Spirit, take my thoughts captive."*

I opened to Philippians 4 and made myself read each truth *out loud.* Slowly. Again. Then I wrote down my biggest fear—and what Scripture said about it.

By noon, my mind was clearer—not because I forced positivity, but because I invited truth.

 Supporting Scriptures to Renew the Mind:

2. **Romans 12:2 (ESV)**

   "Be transformed by the renewing of your mind."

   You can't think your way into peace—you must be transformed.

3. **Philippians 4:8 (NIV)**

"Whatever is true... noble... pure... think about such things."

 Your peace is often tied to your focus.

4. **2 Corinthians 10:5 (CSB)**

   "We take every thought captive to obey Christ."

    You can't control every thought—but you don't have to keep every one that comes.

Elijah and the Overthinking Prophet

After calling down fire on Mount Carmel, Elijah fled in fear and sat under a broom tree, saying:

"I have had enough, Lord. Take my life." — 1 Kings 19:4

God didn't scold him. He fed him, let him rest, and then whispered **truth** to his weary mind.

Sometimes the most spiritual thing you can do is **pause, rest, and receive truth** to replace the lies circling in your mind.

⚔ Spiritual Warfare Teaching:

Thought Replacement, Not Just Thought Resistance

The enemy plants seeds of:

- Catastrophizing
- Overgeneralization
- Shame-based loops

- "What if…" traps

The Spirit counters with:

- **Truth-centered thinking**
- **Peaceful presence**
- **Renewed neural pathways through prayer and repetition**

The battlefield is not your feelings—it's your thoughts. And your thoughts are **not your identity**.

🏹 How to Fight Back:

1. **Pray Before You Think.**
   Begin each morning by surrendering your thoughts to God—*before* they begin to spiral.

2. **Replace, Don't Just Resist.**
   When anxious thoughts arise, don't just say "stop"—speak the opposite truth. Turn *"What if I fail?"* into *"God is with me even if I stumble."*

3. **Meditate on the Word—Out Loud.**
   Silence the mental noise with spoken truth. Hearing it reinforces believing it.

4. **Create a "Truth List."**
   Write down 5 Scriptures that counter your top 5 anxious thoughts—and keep them visible (mirror, phone, fridge).

Faith in Action: "Anointed Thought Tracker"

Start this 5-day challenge:

1. **Morning:**
   Pray: *"Holy Spirit, anoint my mind today. Let me think like You."*

2. **Midday Check-In:**
   Ask: *"What have I been thinking about the most today?"*

3. **Evening Reflection:**
   Write down one anxious thought + the truth that replaces it.

Repeat. Train your mind through surrender, not striving.

 Warfare Prayer

Holy Spirit,

You are the Counselor and Teacher. I surrender my thoughts to You. Every worry, every mental loop, every fearful image—I lay them at Your feet. Renew my thoughts and heal every distorted pattern rooted in fear, trauma, or lies. Anoint my mind with clarity, calm, and spiritual insight. Help me think thoughts that glorify You.

Let Your Word be the filter for every belief I carry. Anoint my mind with peace. Saturate my thought life with truth. Let me think thoughts that are aligned with heaven, not hell. Rewire what anxiety has built. Transform my mind through Your presence. In Jesus' name, Amen.

Scripture Declarations

- ❖ "I have the mind of Christ."
- ❖ "My thoughts are not ruled by fear, but by truth."
- ❖ "Every anxious thought is taken captive and made to obey Christ."
- ❖ I reject toxic patterns and embrace holy thinking.

 Journal Prompt

What's one recurring anxious thought you want God to transform? What truth can you speak over it right now?

Group Reflection Questions

1. What kinds of thought patterns often lead you into anxiety?
2. How is "renewing the mind" different from trying to "stay positive"?
3. What can you do practically this week to invite the Holy Spirit into your thought life?

CHAPTER 14

WHEN YOU'RE ANXIOUS FOR OTHERS

Intercession as a Shield

Primary Verse:

"Cast all your anxiety on Him because He cares for you."

— 1 Peter 5:7 (NIV)

Introduction: When Worry Isn't About You

Sometimes the heaviest anxiety isn't what's happening *to* us—it's what's happening to those we love.

You carry:

- The weight of your children's choices
- The burden of your spouse's emotional pain
- The fear of losing someone you can't imagine living without

You lie awake wondering, *What if I can't fix it? What if they never change? What if something happens?*

But here's the truth: **Worry doesn't protect people—prayer does.**

God never asked us to carry burdens for others alone. He invites us to **intercede**—to *stand in the gap*—and to trust His heart when ours feels helpless.

⚜ Theological Insight:

Intercession Is Not Helplessness—It's Heavenly Power

The Bible calls Jesus our **intercessor** (Romans 8:34). He continually prays on our behalf.

Intercession isn't passive pity. It's **active partnership** with the Spirit.

It's laying someone on the altar—not out of fear, but in **faith**.

"The prayer of a righteous person is powerful and effective." — James 5:16 (NIV)

You're not powerless. When you pray, heaven moves.

✖ Common Lies We Often Live With:

- "If I don't worry about them, I must not care enough."
- "Their safety and success depends on me."
- "If I stop trying, everything will fall apart."
- "God isn't doing enough—I need to help more."
- "If I don't carry this, no one else will."

⚠ *These lies disguise fear as love and control as compassion.*

Carrying Others Was Breaking Me

There was a season I tried to fix everything—counsel everyone, protect everyone, pray for everyone… while secretly falling apart.

Anxiety disguised itself as **responsibility**.

But God showed me that I wasn't their Savior—I was their servant. And sometimes the most powerful thing I could do was release them in prayer.

Intercession became my shield against codependency and despair.

Letting Go When I Couldn't Hold On

I remember the nights I couldn't sleep—staring at the ceiling, heart racing, terrified that a call would come saying she was gone. My grandmother meant everything to me. The thought of losing her felt like the world would collapse.

Every vibration from my phone made me flinch. Every silence stretched like an ache. I prayed—but if I'm honest, it wasn't peace-filled prayer. It was begging. Bargaining. Pleading with God to keep her here a little longer.

The anxiety became constant. I was worn out emotionally, physically, spiritually. One night, somewhere between exhaustion and surrender, I opened my Bible and read 1 Peter 5:7: **"Cast all your anxiety on Him because He cares for you."**

I'd read it before—but this time, it landed differently. In the stillness, I felt the Holy Spirit speak to my heart:

"If I care this deeply for you… don't you believe I care for her too?"

I broke. The tears came, not from fear, but from release. That night, I whispered, "God, I give her to You. I can't carry this anymore. She was Yours before she was mine."

Peace didn't come because the outcome changed. Peace came because I *surrendered* what I was never meant to carry alone.

Supporting Scriptures for Interceding Through Anxiety:

1. **1 Peter 5:7 (NIV)**

   "Cast all your anxiety on Him because He cares for you."

    God doesn't just care about you—He cares about what's burdening you.

2. **Romans 8:26 (ESV)**

   "The Spirit helps us in our weakness... with groanings too deep for words."

    Even when you don't know what to pray, the Spirit fills the gap.

3. **Philippians 4:6–7 (NLT)**

   "Pray about everything... and you will experience God's peace..."

    Prayer isn't just for peace—it's where peace begins.

Job

Job lost everything. His grief was unspeakable. But after his restoration began, notice what God instructed:

"My servant Job will pray for you, and I will accept his prayer..." — Job 42:8

Job's intercession for his friends was **key to his healing**. Sometimes when you're anxious for others, **your prayers are unlocking something for you too.**

Moses – Standing in the Gap for a Nation

Few figures in Scripture embody the heart of intercession like Moses. Time and again, he carried not just the burden of leadership but the emotional weight of the people he led. Their rebellion, complaints, and spiritual blindness could have easily led him to wash his hands of them. Instead, Moses chose to stand in the gap— fighting for them in prayer even when they didn't deserve it.

One of the most powerful examples comes in **Exodus 32**, after the Israelites made a golden calf while Moses was receiving the Ten Commandments on Mount Sinai. God's anger burned, and He told Moses He was ready to destroy them and start over.

But Moses did something remarkable:

"But Moses sought the favor of the Lord his God. 'Lord,' he said, 'why should your anger burn against your people... Turn from your fierce anger; relent and do not bring disaster on your people.'"
— Exodus 32:11–12 (NIV)

He **interceded**, reminding God of His covenant, His promises, and His mercy. And God relented.

This wasn't a one-time act. Moses often prayed for the people when they were rebellious, afraid, or disobedient. His prayers became a **spiritual shield** that preserved them when they deserved judgment.

Why it matters: Intercession is not passive—it is spiritual warfare. Like Moses, we are called to carry others to God, especially when anxiety tries to crush our hearts on their behalf. Whether it's a child, spouse, friend, or nation, your prayers matter. You may not have control over their circumstances, but you have access to the God who does.

Spiritual Warfare Teaching:
Intercession Breaks the Enemy's Hold

The enemy uses relational anxiety to:

- Create fear-based control
- Distract you from your own peace
- Convince you you're responsible for outcomes

But intercession does the opposite:

- It releases control to God
- Covers others with divine protection
- Aligns your heart with God's will—not just your will for them

How to Fight Back:

1. **Pray Before You Speak.**
   Before trying to solve or comfort, intercede. Let your first instinct be heavenward, not human-centered.

2. **Use God's Word as a Covering.**
   Instead of rehearsing fear, declare promises. Speak Scripture over their name—daily.

3. **Release Control Daily.**
   Write their name in your journal, circle it in prayer, and say: *"God, they're Yours. Help me love without carrying the weight."*

4. **Don't Neglect Your Own Peace.**
   Intercession is not spiritual burnout. It's love that prays without losing your own soul in the process.

Faith in Action: The 3-Part Intercession Framework

1. **Name the Burden:**
   Who or what are you worried about right now?

2. **Pray the Promise:**
   Find a Scripture to speak over that person/situation (e.g., Isaiah 54:13 for children).

3. **Release the Outcome:**
   Declare aloud: *"Lord, I release _____ to You. I trust You to care more than I can."*

Warfare Prayer

Father,

You see the ones I love. You know the burdens I carry on their behalf. Today, I lay them at Your feet. I will not carry what You did not assign. I intercede with faith—not fear. Let Your will be done. Cover them with grace. Speak to them when I cannot. Reach them where I cannot go. And give me peace that only comes from knowing You are in control.
In Jesus' name, Amen.

 Scripture Declarations

- ❖ "I cast my anxiety on God because He cares for me—and those I love."
- ❖ "I am not the Savior—I am an intercessor.
- ❖ "My prayers create spiritual covering, not control."
- ❖ "I will not be crushed by the burdens I carry for others—God carries them better."

 Journal Prompt

Who or what have you been anxious about lately?
What would it look like to release them into God's hands today?

Group Reflection Questions

1. How can intercession become a shield against anxiety for loved ones?

2. What are some warning signs you're carrying responsibility instead of surrendering it?

3. What's one promise from Scripture you can begin praying over someone you're worried about?

Final Encouragement: You Are Armed with Peace

– You Are Armed with Peace

Scripture: "Peace I leave with you; my peace I give you. I do not give to you as the world gives. Do not let your hearts be troubled and do not be afraid." – John 14:27 (NIV)

You've walked through these pages, faced the shadows of anxiety, and discovered that God's peace is not fragile—it is fortified by the blood of Christ. Every fear you've faced is an opportunity for His glory to shine brighter. Every anxious thought is a moment to take captive and make it obedient to Christ.

Your armor is not forged in your own strength—it is anchored in the Cross. There, Jesus bore every fear, every anxious whisper, every restless night, and declared, "It is finished." That means your fight has already been won.

So, walk boldly. Not because fear will never knock again, but because you now know how to answer—with the Sword of the Spirit, the Shield of Faith, and the unshakable peace of God.

Prayer of Commissioning:

Lord, thank You for arming me with Your peace. As I go forward, help me stand firm when fear calls my name. Let my life reflect the victory You purchased on the Cross. May my words speak life, my thoughts align with Your truth, and my heart remain anchored in Your presence. I am armed, I am covered, and I am Yours. In Jesus' name, Amen.

Invitation to Christ:
Your Victory Begins at the Cross

You've read about the armor. You've seen the spiritual battle. But none of it matters if you don't know the One who gives the victory.

Right now, if you've been living in fear, fighting battles alone, or running from peace—there is hope. His name is Jesus.

He's not distant.
He's not angry with you.
He's not waiting for you to "get it all together."

He's standing with open arms, ready to give you rest, redemption, and a new beginning.

Scripture says:

"Come to Me, all who are weary and burdened, and I will give you rest."
— Matthew 11:28 (NIV)

That rest, that peace, begins with a relationship with Jesus Christ. Salvation is not about religion—it's about surrender. It's about receiving the gift He already paid for on the cross.

Today is your day.

A Simple Prayer of Salvation

If you're ready to begin a new life in Christ, pray this from your heart:

*"**Lord Jesus**, I admit that I need You. I've tried to do life on my own and I've come up empty. I confess my sins and I ask You to forgive me. I believe You died for me and rose again so I could be free. Today, I give You my heart. I make You my Savior and my Lord. Fill me with Your peace. Clothe me with Your righteousness. Teach me to walk in victory. In Jesus' name, Amen."*

❓ What Happens Next?

If you just prayed that prayer, **welcome to the family of God**. The angels are rejoicing—and so are we (Luke 15:10). You don't walk this journey alone. Here's what you can do next:

- **Get a Bible** and begin reading the Gospel of John.
- **Talk to God every day**—just like you would a friend. That's prayer.
- **Find a Bible-teaching church** where you can grow in faith.
- **Tell someone** about your decision—share your testimony.

You've just made the most important decision of your life—and the best is yet to come.

You are no longer anxious—you are anchored. No longer lost—you are found. You are now armed with peace.

Spiritual Tools & Resources

Equip yourself daily with these tools designed to strengthen your spirit, renew your mind, and guard your heart:

• Daily Armor Checklist

A practical checklist to "put on the full armor of God" (Ephesians 6:10–18) each morning.

• Morning Scripture Declarations

Start your day by speaking truth over your mind and heart. Declare God's Word to set the tone for peace and boldness.

• Evening Renewal Prayer

Wind down each night with a short guided prayer to release the day's worries and receive restful peace.

• Scripture Memory Cards

Portable truth cards for memorizing key verses—carry God's promises with you wherever you go.

• Worship Playlist for Peace

A curated list of calming, spirit-lifting worship songs to play during devotion, prayer, or anxious moments.

• Guided Breath & Prayer Journal Template

Combine biblical meditation with breath prayers and journaling prompts to realign your heart with God's truth.

Personal Self-Assessment

Use the following checklist to evaluate where anxiety may be showing up in your life. Mark any statements that resonate:

- I often overthink conversations or decisions.
- I avoid stillness because it makes me feel uneasy.
- I feel responsible for things outside my control.
- I struggle to sleep due to worry or fear.
- I replay past events and 'what-ifs' frequently.
- I fear being a burden to others if I'm honest.

If three or more of these statements describe you, consider implementing daily spiritual rhythms from this book.

Scripture Declarations

Declare these truths daily over your mind and spirit:

- *"I have the mind of Christ."*

  — 1 Corinthians 2:16

- *"I am anxious for nothing."*

  — Philippians 4:6

- *"God is not the author of confusion, but of peace."*

  — 1 Corinthians 14:33

- *"I walk by faith, not by fear."*

  — 2 Corinthians 5:7

- *"Perfect love casts out fear."*

  — 1 John 4:18

- *"The Lord is my Shepherd; I shall not want."*

  — Psalm 23:1

- *"You will keep in perfect peace those whose minds are steadfast."*

  — Isaiah 26:3

- *"Greater is He who is in me than he who is in the world."*

  — 1 John 4:4

- *"I have not been given a spirit of fear, but of power, love, and a sound mind."*

  — *2 Timothy 1:7*

- *"When I am afraid, I put my trust in You."*

  — *Psalm 56:3*

- *"No weapon formed against me shall prosper."*

  — *Isaiah 54:17*

- *"The joy of the Lord is my strength."*

  — *Nehemiah 8:10*

- *"I cast all my anxiety on Him because He cares for me."*

  — *1 Peter 5:7*

Intercessory Prayer Prompts

Use these prompts when praying for loved ones experiencing anxiety:

- "Lord, calm their storm and speak peace over their mind."

- "Surround them with support, love, and truth."

- "Protect their thoughts and renew their hope."

- "I release them into Your care today, trusting Your plan."

- "Holy Spirit, be their counselor and comfort."

Scripture Index by Chapter

A selection of key scriptures used throughout this book:

Chapter 1: The Belt of Truth

- John 8:31–32 – Truth will set you free
- 2 Corinthians 10:5 – Take every thought captive
- Psalm 119:160 – The sum of Your word is truth

Chapter 2: The Breastplate of Righteousness

- Isaiah 61:10 – Clothed with garments of salvation
- 2 Corinthians 5:21 – We are the righteousness of God
- Proverbs 4:23 – Guard your heart

Chapter 3: The Shoes of Peace

- Isaiah 26:3 – Perfect peace whose mind is on You
- Philippians 4:7 – Peace that passes understanding
- Romans 10:15 – Feet fitted with the gospel of peace

Chapter 4: The Shield of Faith

- Ephesians 6:16 – Shield of faith extinguishes flaming arrows
- Hebrews 11:1 – Faith is confidence in what we hope for
- 1 John 5:4 – Victory through faith

Chapter 5: The Helmet of Salvation

- 1 Thessalonians 5:8 – Hope of salvation as a helmet
- Romans 12:2 – Renewing of the mind
- Isaiah 26:3 – Mind stayed on You brings peace

Chapter 6: The Sword of the Spirit

- Hebrews 4:12 – Word of God is living and active
- Matthew 4:4 – Man shall not live on bread alone
- Isaiah 55:11 – God's Word will not return void

Chapter 7: Praying in the Spirit

- Ephesians 6:18 – Pray in the Spirit on all occasions
- Romans 8:26 – The Spirit helps us in our weakness
- Philippians 4:6 – By prayer and petition present requests

Chapter 8: After the Battle

- Exodus 14:14 – The Lord will fight for you
- Psalm 30:5 – Weeping may endure for a night
- Isaiah 40:31 – Those who wait on the Lord renew strength

Chapter 9: The Voice Behind the Fear

- John 10:27 – My sheep hear my voice
- Romans 8:15 – Spirit of adoption, not fear
- 1 John 4:1 – Test the spirits

Chapter 10: The Armor in the Midnight Hour

- Psalm 119:62 – I rise at midnight to give thanks
- Acts 16:25 – Paul and Silas prayed at midnight
- Exodus 12:29 – God moved at midnight

Chapter 11: Breaking the Cycle

- Exodus 20:5–6 – Generational consequences
- Galatians 5:1 – Stand firm in freedom
- Isaiah 43:19 – A new thing springs forth

Chapter 12: From Anxious to Anchored

- Hebrews 6:19 – Hope is an anchor for the soul
- Matthew 11:28 – Come to Me and I will give rest
- Psalm 62:5–6 – My hope comes from Him

Chapter 13: The Anointed Mind

- 1 Corinthians 2:16 – We have the mind of Christ
- Philippians 2:5 – Let this mind be in you
- Romans 8:6 – Mind governed by Spirit is life and peace

Chapter 14: When You're Anxious for Others

- Philippians 4:6 – Let your requests be known to God
- James 1:5 – Ask God for wisdom
- Ezekiel 22:30 – Stand in the gap

About the Author

(Dr. Derrick Washington)

Dr. Derrick Washington is a passionate minister, author, and dynamic speaker whose life and message center on hope, healing, and victory through Jesus Christ. With a unique blend of pastoral compassion and academic excellence, he ministers to hearts while equipping minds with biblical truth.

Having personally navigated seasons of chronic illness, the loss of loved ones, and the intense battles of spiritual warfare, Dr. Washington writes and speaks from a place of lived experience. His words are not merely theories—they are forged in the crucible of faith under fire. Each page of his work carries the authenticity of someone who has seen God's faithfulness in the darkest valleys and can testify to His sustaining grace.

Dr. Washington holds a Doctorate in Organizational Leadership with a concentration in Information Systems and Technology, blending leadership insight with technical expertise. Ordained in ministry, he has dedicated his life to helping others rise above fear, anxiety, and spiritual defeat. His teaching style is both relatable and deeply rooted in Scripture, making complex biblical truths accessible to everyday believers.

Whether standing behind a pulpit, leading a small group, or writing for a global audience, his mission is clear: to equip people with the armor of God, inspire them to walk boldly in their calling, and remind them that no battle is too great when fought from a place of victory in Christ.

Connect the Journey

You've taken a powerful step toward living free from anxiety's grip. Don't stop here—keep walking in truth and strength.

Read More in the Journey to Victory Series:

- *From Trials to Testimony: When the Test Becomes the Story That Sets Others Free*
- *Walking in Victory: Living Beyond the Storm*
- *Faith Over Fear: Armor for the Anxious – Winning the Battle Within*

Stay Connected:
◉ **Website:** InspiringFaithByDW.com
▨ **Join My Email List:** Get weekly encouragement and free study resources delivered to your inbox.
▦ **Social Media:** @InspiringFaithDW (Instagram, Facebook)

Help Others Find Freedom:
If this book has impacted your life, please take a moment to leave a review on Amazon. Your testimony might be the key that unlocks someone else's breakthrough.

You've fought the battle. Now help someone else win theirs